A DICTIONARY OF

AUSTRALIAN
SLANG

A DICTIONARY OF

AUSTRALIAN SLANG

SIDNEY J. BAKER

With an introduction by
KEITH DUNSTAN

VIKING O'NEIL

Viking O'Neil
Penguin Books Australia Ltd
487 Maroondah Highway, PO Box 257
Ringwood, Victoria 3134, Australia
Penguin Books Ltd
Harmondsworth, Middlesex, England
Viking Penguin Inc.
40 West 23rd Street, New York, N.Y. 10010, U.S.A.
Penguin Books Canada Ltd
2801 John Street, Markham, Ontario, Canada L3R 1B4
Penguin Books (N.Z.) Ltd
182-190 Wairau Road, Auckland 10, New Zealand

First published 1959
New edition published by Lloyd O'Neil Pty Ltd 1982
Reprinted 1983, 1986
This edition published by Penguin Books Australia Ltd 1988
Copyright © Dictionary text: Suzanne Baker, 1982
Copyright © Introduction: Keith Dunstan, 1982

Produced by Viking O'Neil
56 Claremont Street, South Yarra, Victoria 3141, Australia
A division of Penguin Books australia Ltd

Typeset in Australia
Printed and bound in Hong Kong through Bookbuilders Ltd

National Library of Australia
Cataloguing-in-Publication data

Baker, Sidney J. (Sidney John), 1912-1976.
A dictionary of Australian slang.

ISBN 0 670 90086 9.

1. English language — Australia — Slang
— Dictionaries, I. Title.

427'.994

INTRODUCTION

Is there a dinkum Australian language? Sidney J. Baker has proved it over and over again. You notice it particularly far from home, say in Kangaroo Valley, London's Earls Court. That's when Australians show their nationalism. They burn gum leaves in the grate for the aroma of the eucalyptus and they bandy round vintage Ockerisms that they would never use at home, like 'bonzer', 'goodoh' and 'don't come the raw prawn with me, mate'.

When television conquered Australia in 1956 most of us thought it would mean the end of the Australian language. At one stage among the great barrage of American programs there were twenty-two different series of Westerns with all their slang straight out of Arizona, Colorado and, worst of all, down-town Burbank.

If one believed in Marshal McLuhan's theory of the global village, how could any Australian slang survive? But it has survived and much of it has proved extraordinarily resilient.

You listen to a dinkum Australian in full cry and he needs a little interpretation in a place like Market Street, San Francisco. Take a line like this: 'What a two bob lair you turned out to be, trying to do a bit of good for yourself with a drak sheila like that. Talk about crook, I don't reckon she even had the full quid'.

Most of those expressions are aged but you still hear them. The truth is that if you move about the United States and even use simple words like 'togs' for swimming costume, 'tucker' for food, and 'whinge' for complain, or should you mention 'doing your lolly', the answer will be a puzzled 'Huh?'

It is also easy to get oneself into trouble. Some thirty years ago I was working in New York. In the office there was a very pretty nineteen-year-old secretary and she came from one of the best families on Park Avenue.

She approached me one day and complained that she was being miserably underpaid by our Australian newspaper. Indeed the money was so poor she could hardly afford to dress herself.

I was embarrassed. I had only been there two days. 'I'm sorry', I said, 'What do you get for a screw?'

She looked at me in horror, and sobbing she left the room.

Back in those days 'screw' was the honourable and useful Australian word for salary.

Now, thirty years later, we are still having problems. Early in 1982 the director of the Miami Film Festival in Florida wrote to Mike Harris, the representative of the Australian Film Commission in Los Angeles. He said that he was anxious to show Australian feature films at the festival. He would be very happy to receive some recent films from the commission, but he could only show them under one condition. They must come with English subtitles.

Mike Harris wrote back tactfully that English was the normal spoken language in Australia, but if some of the terms did seem strange he could provide a glossary.

I have always felt that if there is a National Trust for cherished Australian buildings then there should also be a National Trust for great Australian words and expressions. If we give our famous buildings gradings such as A, 'to be preserved at all costs'; B, 'highly favoured for preservation' and, say, C for 'noteworthy', then we should do the same for our great expressions.

'Don't come the raw prawn' is an obvious A. 'Nothing but a whinging old wowser' is worthy of a double A and there are some like 'shivoo' which obviously call for desperate restoration work.

'Aving a bit of a shivoo tonight are you mate?' Shivoo, the name for a party, was in common use everywhere when I was a boy. Now it is in sad need of rehabilitation. It's as rare as the Tasmanian tiger.

'Bonzer', the Australian word for true excellence, also is in peril. Its variation 'boshter' is common enough as used by C. J. Dennis in *The Sentimental Bloke*, but I have never heard anyone say it.

The Sentimental Bloke himself, also was in regular trouble for 'stoushin' Johns', a vintage term for fighting with the police. Yes, 'having a bit of a stoush' is certainly worth a B.

Some of them are beyond repair. Even a 'Word National Trust' could not restore the damage done to 'sonky' for stupid. I can just dimly remember my parents talking of children as young 'snoozers'. Nobody does now.

The same parents did have a 'snout' on this and that when they were displeased, and what about the various terms for a prostitute: 'endless belt', 'Mallee root', 'ferry', 'chromo', 'lowheel'. All gone.

The United States has conquered. When we think of a prostitute now we are more likely to think of a hooker. Yet here and there we have resisted the American invasion. Despite John Wayne and all the Western movies, we don't have rustlers. Our term is far more colourful. Such thieves indulge in cattle duffing or poddy dodging.

And is it too late to save 'yonnie'? Could we give it an A? The very word evokes memories of a far off boyhood. Back in the 1930s, every pebble was a yonnie. A yonnie was something that you fired off in your ging, your catapult.

Boys more often made their own toys then and maybe the greatest of all pleasures was creating a really worthwhile ging and skipping yonnies across the surface of the Yarra.

So many dictionaries have all the charm of a telephone

book. Sidney J. Baker, with his sly sense of humour, created a dictionary that has to be read. One of his techniques was to create the broadest Australian slang phrase, then to give it meaning with a solemn, perhaps even pompous line of English. The contrast inevitably is charming. For example, we learn that 'to perve' is 'to extract pleasure from looking at her, especially if she is scantily dressed on a beach'. The 'dinkum oil' is 'the truth, information of strict authenticity'.

Sidney Baker had an ear for Australian speech. He could sense at once the true indigenous local dialogue. So often it comes in a pattern, repeated over and over like a script for a play.

When an Australian says, 'Ow ya goin?' there is the choice of three replies. One can say: (1) Not bad, ow's yerself? (2) Good as gold. (3) Carn complain. Probably (1) and (3) are the perfect replies. It is in the Australian character never to concede too much. Even if you are feeling very good or very bad you do not admit it.

However, if you are boasting of sexual prowess then that is a different matter. Sidney J. Baker, in this book, tells us of that wonderful line 'Getting any?' He says 'It is usually addressed by man to man and enquires whether the listener has been achieving amorous successes of late'.

He has a choice of three replies: (1) Climbing trees to get away from it! (2) Got to swim under water to dodge it! (3) So busy I've had to put a man on!

Sidney J. Baker never received the honours he deserved. It is possible to learn more about Australia from him than from almost any other writer. His book *The Australian Language*, first published in 1945, is one of the most important of all Australian books.

Those of us – let us not use the word writer – those of us who are word mechanics, find Baker, along with Fowler, Roget and the Oxford Dictionary, the indispensable works of reference on the bookshelf.

Sidney J. Baker was a walking library of knowledge. When he was producing these immensely useful books he was a sub-editor on the *Sydney Morning Herald*. Whenever I was in trouble, couldn't find the right Australian word, or couldn't get the right nuance of meaning, I would call him on the telephone.

Patiently he would pass out his information free of charge. The last time I called him was to ask the origin of 'Ocker'. Now Ocker was not in his dictionary, yet of all the new slang words it seemed so richly descriptive.

An Ocker was an Ocker. It described so perfectly those characters one saw and heard on the Paddington Hill or behind the goals at Victoria Park. An Ocker was the quintessential Australian.

He was not going to swear to this theory but Sid Baker thought Ocker came from Oscar. There was a time when all Oscars were called Ocker, he said. And Oscar, particularly to schoolboys, seemed an outlandish, slightly peculiar name. So Ockers were a bit odd and eventually the name came to suit all of us. The Ocker or odd people.

He died soon after.

Keith Dunstan

AUSTRALIAN
SLANG
DICTIONARY

THIS list of Australian words and phrases has two aims: to provide definitions for several hundred Australian terms used earlier, and, more important, to offer evidence of the immense variety of slang, colloquialism and idiom found in Australia to-day.

It should not be even fleetingly thought that what follows is a complete list of our slang. On the contrary, it is only about a third of the many expressions that have emerged in Australia, either as adaptations of English terms or as indigenous inventions.

Apart from a relatively few examples about which clarification will possibly be needed by newcomers to this country, I have eliminated most of our obsolescent or obsolete slang. The old terms and phrases that remain are mainly examples occurring in our literature and may, hence, be encountered by readers of that literature. Localised slang, and there is a mass of it, has been almost entirely ignored. So also with craft slang and a good deal of our sectional slang — as used, for example, by children. Nonce-words are out — even recent neologisms that may in due course acquire a firm place in our speech. Of the many hundreds of words and phrases developed by Service personnel in World Wars I and II only examples remaining in general use to-day have been preserved. And only the most commonly used slang terms for our flora and fauna will be found here.

What remains is largely the solid core of Australian English, known and used throughout the nation. Much of it is no longer slang, but standard terms that can probably never be displaced.

Except in a few cases, I have refrained from offering explanations about the origins of the items in this list because of the space those explanations would have occupied. Thereby, of course, a great deal is lost, for many of the terms that follow have fascinating histories.

Even so, what emerges from this vocabulary is important in letting us see the developing nature of the Australian character. Perhaps, in a way, that is the main point. This character is far from being rigid and static. When, the best part of a generation ago, I began to investigate Australian slang, a large part of it was clearly derived from the Australian's life and experiences in the bush or outback. Now, much of that traditional idiom is dying or dead. Instead, we see a remarkable growth in urban slang. The voice of our inland is no longer the main source of linguistic novelty in Australia. Nearly everything new to be said in our bush or outback has been said. It should not be thought that this is entirely a recent development. Its beginnings were evident around 1900, but as vast populations have concentrated in our major cities its strength has become increasingly obvious. Yet, even if the nature of our slang and idiom has changed, a constant factor remains. This is the remarkable Australian flair for linguistic innovation.

In "Australian Democracy" (1958), A. F. Davies says: "The characteristic talent of Australians is not for improvisation, nor even for republican manners, it is for bureaucracy." Perhaps he is partly right, but my own view is that our greatest talent is for idiomatic invention. It is a manifestation of our vitality and restless imagination. Whereas much of our early idiom was formerly regarded as the natural product of human experience in a unique environment, it is now clear that the environment served primarily to provide an outlet for our word-making enthusiasm. With our change of focus from outback to city, our capacity for inventing new words and

There is every reason for expecting it to continue to
thrive robustly.

Abbreviations

adj.	adjective
Aust.	Australia, Australian
cf.	compare
e.g.	for example
esp.	especially
i.e.	that is
n.	noun
obs.	obsolete
orig.	originally
q.v.	which see
sl.	slang
v.	verb

A

abo: Aboriginal, n. or adj. **abos,** aborigines (not aboes).
Aboriginal Sunday: An occasion instigated by the
National Missionary Council and observed in many
Protestant Churches with "special addresses on
Australian aborigines."
ace, on one's: Alone, on one's own. Esp. criminal sl.
acid on, put the: To seek a favour (from someone); to ask
(an employer) for a rise in wages; to seek a loan; to
bring pressure to bear on.
act, bung on an: See **bung,** 2. cf. **stack on an act.**
African: A tailor-made cigarette.
Africa speaks: Cheap fortified wine.
afto: See **arvo.**
age-cast (of a sheep): Of poor value because of advancing
years. A **cast-for-age** ewe is about seven years old,
which is regarded as too old for good breeding. 2.
A cow, aged nine years or more, not useful for good
breeding. A horse over seven years old is **aged.**

alberts: Toe or foot rags worn by tramps or swagmen of low degree.

All Blacks: New Zealand representative Rugby Union footballers.

all laired up: Flashily dressed; dressed for some special occasion. cf. **lair.** Also, **all mockered up,** used similarly.

all-upper: A punter who bets "all up" on a number of horse or greyhound races.

all wet: Silly, foolish.

alley: A two-up school.

(**Alphabeticisms:** The many examples include **A.B.C.,** Australian Broadcasting Commission; **A.C.T.,** Aust. Capital Territory; **A.J.C.,** Aust. Jockey Club; **A.L.P.,** Aust. Labour Party; **C.P.,** Country Party; **D.L.P.,** Democratic Labour Party; **G.P.S.,** Great Public Schools; **N.G.,** New Guinea; **N.S.W.,** New South Wales; **N.Z.,** New Zealand; **N.T.** Northern Territory; **O.T.,** Overland Telegraph; **P.P.,** Pastures Protection, mainly used in country as in **P.P. Board; Q.,** Queensland; **S.A.,** South Aust.; **T.,** Tasmania; **V.,** Victoria; **W.A.,** Western Aust.)

also ran: A person who is a failure; one who accomplishes little or nothing in any competitive activity. See **no-hoper.**

amster: A trickster's confederate; a sideshowman's decoy. Also, **amsterdam,** by rhyme on **ram** (q.v.). Criminal sl.

animal: A contemptuous term for an objectionable person.

ant, v.: See **white ant.**

Anzac: A member of the Australian and New Zealand Army Corps in World War I; since applied to any Aust. or New Zealand serviceman, but mainly to soldiers. Whence, **bronzed Anzac,** an ironical allusion to such a serviceman, often used by the servicemen themselves.

Apple Island, the: Tasmania. Whence, **Apple Islander,** a Tasmanian.

apron: The neck fold of a merino ram.

argue the toss: To dispute an order or a decision.

aroo! Goodbye!

arsey: Lucky. See **tinny.**

artichoke: A debauched old woman.

article: As for next.

article, the dinkum: A genuine object or person. See **dinkum.**

artist: One who indulges in excesses, e.g., **bilge artist, booze artist, bull artist, gip artist.**

art union: A lottery in which the prizes are in kind, not money. However, in N.Z. money prizes are offered in art unions.

arvo: Afternoon; usually in the form **this arvo,** or **s'arvo,** this afternoon. Also, **afto.**

auntie! don't be: Don't be stupid or silly! By transference from **don't be Uncle Willy!** a rhyme on "silly."

Aussie: Australia; an Australian.

Aussieland: Australia. Whence, **Aussielander,** an Australian.

Aussie rules: The type of football known as **Australian Rules** (q.v.).

Australia: Many derivatives of this word are Aust. in origin, e.g., **Australianism,** an Aust. expression; **Australiana,** a collection of Aust. historical and other records; **Australia Day,** a national holiday falling on January 26 each year or on the Monday immediately following (also called **Anniversary Day**); **White Australia Policy,** a Federal policy designed to exclude coloured migrants, whence, **White Australia** and **keep Australia white!**

Australian Rules: A code of football developed in the 1850s and particularly popular in Victoria, South Australia and Western Australia.

Australian terrier: A type of terrier first given recognition in 1909.

Australites: Small, smooth lumps of black glass, presumably meteorites, found in Vic., South Aust. and Western Aust.

Australorp: The utility type of Black Orpington fowl.

awkward as a Chow on a bike: Extremely awkward in behaviour. **Chow** denotes Chinaman.

B

back: Used esp. in the phrases **get on someone's back,** to bully or harass, to urge someone on; **be on someone's back,** to be "standing over" someone; and the impatient order, **Get off my back!**

back of beyond: The remote inland country. Also, **back o' beyond.**

back of Bourke: Remote inland country. Mainly N.S.W. sl.

backblocker: A resident of the bush or outback. **Backblockser** was formerly used, but now obs.

backblocks: Sparsely inhabited country remote from a capital. Whence, **backblock,** adj.

backer-up: The accomplice of a ginger (q.v.). Criminal sl.

backing dog: A sheepdog that will run across the backs of sheep to aid mustering or droving. Rural sl.

bad, not: A utility term covering all shades of meaning from excellent to fairly good or passable.

bag, in the (of a racehorse or racing greyhound): Not intended to win.

bagman's gazette: A non-existent publication quoted as a source of rumour, esp. in the country. cf. **drover's guide.**

bagswinger: A bookmaker. 2. A prostitute who walks the streets in search of clients. Whence, **swing a bag,** be a streetwalker.

bail: A framework for securing a cow's head at milking time. Whence, **to bail up** (a cow), to secure a cow's head in a bail. See next:

bail up: To hold up and rob. Orig. a bushranging term, dating from before 1844. Whence, to corner a person; to accost someone. Also, **bail-up,** n., orig. a hold-up by bushrangers; later, any demand for money or attention.

baitlayer: A station cook. Rural sl.

balance, v.: To cheat; used esp. of dishonest bookmakers. Whence, **balancer** and **balancing.**

bald as a bandicoot: Completely bald. See **bandicoot.**

ball of muscle, a: A person who is lively, energetic, high-spirited.

Banana City: Brisbane, Q. See next:

Bananaland: Queensland. Whence, **Bananalander, Banana-eater, Bananaman,** a Queenslander.

band: A prostitute. Also, **belt** and **endless belt.**

bander: Soap; by rhyme on "band of hope."

bandicoot: The following phrases linked with the marsupial are self-explanatory, **bald as a bandicoot, barmey as a bandicoot, lousy as a bandicoot, bandy as a bandicoot, miserable as a bandicoot, poor as a bandicoot, not the brains of a bandicoot.**

bandicooting: The practice of stealing tuberous vegetables, esp. potatoes, from the soil without moving the tops.

bangtails: Cattle. Whence, **bangtail muster,** a periodical counting of herds. Rural sl.

banjo: A frying pan; a shoulder of mutton; a shovel. Also, the inevitable nickname of anyone named Pat(t)erson.

bank: As for **doublebank** (q.v.).

banker: A flooded river, running banks high. **To come down a banker** (of a river), to become flooded.

Bappo: A Baptist. See **Congo, Metho, Presbo.**

barber: A hotel keeper; a thief; a tramp.

Barcoo buster: A westerly gale in mid or south Queensland.

Barcoo challenge: To scrape the points of a pair of hand shears on the shearing floor or wall, indicating a challenge for the day's tally. Obs. rural sl. Also, to throw the belly of a fleece over another shearer's head with the same object.

Barcoo rot: Land scurvy. **Barcoo vomit,** another old bush sickness.

bardy: A wood grub. Whence, **starve the bardies!** a W.A. exclamatory phrase similar to **stone the crows!** (q.v.).

barebelly: A sheep without wool on its belly or inner portions of its hind legs. Rural sl.

barney: A row or argument. Also, **to barney,** to argue; **to barney over,** to quarrel.

barrack, v.: To shout or jeer at; to interrupt noisily. Orig. it meant to express vocal displeasure **against** a side or contestant in a sporting event. Now, one can **barrack for,** meaning to support or encourage a side or contestant, as well as **barrack against.** Whence, **barracker** and **barracking.**

barrel: Line of business or interest, as in **right into** (or **up) my barrel,** just what I want or like.

barrow: A Black Maria. 2. As for **barrel.**

barrow, v.: To shear or partly shear a sheep for a shearer. Shed boys sometimes open up or finish a sheep for a shearer, but the practice is generally discouraged.

bash at: An attempt at, e.g., **have a bash at.** Also, **give it a bash.**

bash it up you! A phrase equivalent to "You know where to put it!" or, more modestly, "Go to the devil!"

bat: A whip carried by a horse-rider. Also, **mop** and **stick.**

batch: A small shack or holiday cottage. Also, **bach.**

batcher: A person (usually, but not always, a male) who lives alone. Also, **bacher.** See **hatter.**

bathers: A bathing costume. See **togs.**

battler: Anyone who struggles hard for existence.

Bay, the: Long Bay Jail, Sydney. Also once used for Botany Bay and incorrectly applied to New Holland as a whole.

be your age! Be reasonable! Use your brains!

beer-up: A party; a drinking bout.

belly: Wool shorn from a sheep's belly. Rural sl.

Belyando spew: A rural sickness. Obs. See **Barcoo rot.**

Bengal lancers: Toughs armed with razor blades who made a practice of slashing and robbing victims, esp. in Sydney.

berley: Ground bait used by fishermen to attract fish. 2. Nonsense or humbug, as in **a bit of berley,** deceit or leg-pulling.

bib in: Any interference, any action of a busybody, esp. in the phrases **stick one's bib in, put** (or **push**) **one's bib in.**

bidgee: An alcoholic drink in which methylated spirits is (or was) the main component.

big dish, the: A major betting coup.

big note, v.: To laud, to give exaggerated praise to. Esp. **to big note oneself.**

big smoke: A large city or town.

big twist: An outstanding success, an occasion for the expression of pleasure. cf. **curl the mo.**

bike: A girl or woman who is indiscriminate in granting her favours. Esp. **office bike, town bike.**

bike, get off one's: To become violently angry.

bilge artist: A person addicted to empty talk or bombast.

Billjim: An Australian. Obs.

billabong: A quasi-oasal riverbend, lacking effluence due to siltation, but generally retaining confluence, by which it fills. Many are seasonal in formation.

billy: A tin can in which water is boiled for tea over a camp fire or in which cooking is done. Also, **billy-can** and **billypot.**

binders: Fibres that grow from one staple to another and hold a sheep's fleece together. Rural sl.

binjey: The stomach.

bit hot, a: Unreasonable, beyond the pale of common-sense or justice.

bite: A loan of money; a "prospect" for a loan. Related expressions include **to bite (someone), to bite, chew** or **lug someone's ear** and **earlugger,** a borrower.

bite someone's name: To eat a meal provided by another person. Synonyms include **sign one's hand** and **sign one's name.**

bitumen blonde: An aboriginal girl or woman.

black, adj.: As attached to various names of days, this adj. denotes tragedy or distress, e.g., **black Wednes-**

day, Jan. 9, 1878, a day on which wholesale dismissals of Victorian civil servants occurred; **black Thursday,** Feb. 6, 1851, a day of disastrous bushfires in Victoria; **black Friday,** Jan. 13, 1939, another day of tragic bushfires in Victoria in which 71 lives were lost; **black Saturday,** Dec. 10, 1938, a day of serious bushfires in N.S.W.; **black Sunday,** Feb. 6, 1938, a day on which five people were drowned, 40 rescued unconscious and about 260 other swimmers swept out to sea at Bondi Beach, Sydney, by three receding waves; **black Monday,** Oct. 15, 1945, so-called by planters in N.G. and Papua, when all native labour contracts were cancelled by order of the Aust. Government.

blackbird: A (kidnapped) Polynesian native transported to Queensland for plantation work. Whence, **to blackbird, blackbird catching, blackbirding, blackbirder.** All obs.

black diamond: A type of cicada.

blackfellow: An Aust. aboriginal.

blackfellow's buttons: As for **Australites** (q.v.).

blackfellow's delight: Rum.

black friday: A type of cicada. See note at **green monday.**

black jack: Treacle. 2. A tin pot for boiling tea or cooking, esp. the now almost obs. **quart pot.**

black north-easter: A north-easterly gale, esp. such a gale experienced on Aust. east coast.

black prince: A type of cicada.

blacksmith: A poor cook. Mainly rural sl.

black stump, this side of the: A measure of comprehensiveness or great distance, e.g., the best, worst, finest, rudest, etc., **this side of the black stump.**

black tracker: An aboriginal used by police to track down a lost or wanted person in rough country.

bladder: A type of cicada.

blight: A type of ophthalmia known as **sandy-blight** (q.v.). See also **pink-eye.**

blind country: Closed-in country of colourless type and of little worth.

blind Freddy: A person who is not to be deceived. Mainly used in such statements as "even blind Freddy would see through that," "blind Freddy could pick that one," "it wouldn't fool even blind Freddy."

block, do one's: To become angry or violently excited.

block, do the: To stroll in the central area of Melbourne or Sydney. Rare.

blokery: Men in general.

blow: A stroke with handshears when shearing a sheep.

blow-in: A newcomer at any place; a person who has not yet been accepted by local inhabitants as one of themselves.

bludge, v.: To loaf, to impose on (someone). Orig. to act as a harlot's bully. As n., a period of loafing or of operating some minor racket.

bludger: A loafer or idler, one who imposes on others; a general term of contempt.

bludging: Loafing; the dodging of work or responsibility.

blue: A summons. 2. An error of judgment, a mistake. 3. A fight, esp. in the form **bung on a blue,** begin a fight or dispute. 4. A swagman's bundle or **bluey** (q.v.). 5. Inevitable nickname for any red-haired person.

blue, bet on the: To bet on credit. Also, the rhyme **bet on the Mary Lou.**

blue-tongue: A station rouseabout; a sheep musterer. See **lizard.**

bluey: A bundle, orig. consisting of a blue-coloured blanket with belongings rolled in it, carried by a swagman (q.v.). 2. A summons. See **blue.** 3. A type of cattle dog used in Aust. 4. Nickname for a red-haired person.

board: The floor of a woolshed; the total number of shearers employed in a woolshed. Whence, **boss-of-the-board,** a woolshed overseer.

bob-in: A collection to which each contributor gives a shilling. Also, **two-bob in, deaner-in, zack-in.**

bobby (calf, foal): See **poddy.**

bodgie: The modern Aust. **larrikin** (q.v.). See **widgie.**

body-strike: See **fly-strike.**

boggi (pronounced **bog-eye**): The handpiece of a shearing machine. Rural sl.

bogie: A swimming hole, a bath; a swim or an ablution. Also, **bogiehole, bogiehouse.**

boil-up: A row or argument.

boko: Blind in one eye—applied to man, horse or dog. Rural sl.

bolter's, the: See **haven't the bolter's.**

bomb, n.: Any old car, but esp. a car made in the 1930s. See **brown bomber.**

bomb, v.: To dope a racehorse. See **sting, n.**

bombo: Cheap wine. cf. **plonk.**

bombora: A dangerous area of broken sea water, usually near the base of a cliff where waves break over submerged rocks.

Bondi, go through like a: To hurry, esp. to decamp in a great hurry; to leave a task or obligation on a sudden whim. See **shoot through.** The orig. phrase was **travel like a Bondi tram,** travel at great speed.

bone, v.: To jinx, to bring bad luck to. Also, **to point a bone** at (someone). From the aboriginal practice of pointing or singing a bone.

bong: Dead. This aboriginal term survives now in **to go bung,** to fail, to become bankrupt or ineffective.

bonzer: Good, excellent. Formerly widely used, the word is now rare. So, also, with **bontoger, bontogerino, bonzerino, bonziorie, bonzo** and other derivatives.

boofhead: A fool or simpleton.

boomerang: An aboriginal throwing weapon of wide range in shape and size. Since it is incorrectly assumed that all boomerangs are vested with the property of returning to the thrower, hence 2. That

which returns or which it is intended should be
returned. As v., to return.

boong: An aboriginal. Also a native of New Guinea, and
hence any dark-skinned person.

bootlaces: Narrow strips of skin (from a sheep) cut off
by an inexpert shearer. Rural sl.

booze artist: A habitual drinker; a drunkard.

booze-up: A drinking bout.

borak: Teasing or taunting words. See next:

borak at, poke: To tease, make fun of, chaff (a person).
See **mullock at, poke.**

boshter, bosker: As for **bonzer.** Obs.

boss cocky: Orig. a farmer who employs labour.
Whence, a "top dog," one who has the final say in
an undertaking.

boss-of-the-board: A woolshed manager or overseer.
Also **boss-over-the-board** and **man-over-the-board.**

bot: A germ. 2. A persistent borrower.

bot, have the: To be sick, out of sorts.

bot, to: To borrow money, to "sponge."

Botany wool: Any wool exported from Australia.
Whence, **Botany yarn,** yarn produced from Aust.
wool.

bottle-oh: A collector of empty bottles. Whence, **bottle-
oh's rouseabout,** a nobody.

bottler: First-class, excellent. Also, **bottling.**

boundary rider: An employee of a **station** (q.v.) who
patrols boundaries to prevent the straying of stock
and/or to inspect fences. Whence, **to boundary
ride** and **boundary riding.**

bowser: A petrol pump.

bow the crumpet: (Of an offender in a law-court) to
plead guilty. Also, **nod the nut** and **duck the scone.**
Criminal sl.

bower bird: A petty thief; an inveterate collector of
trivia.

bowyang: A strap or string placed below the knees of a
worker's pants to keep the cuffs off the ground.

box: A mixing of sheep or other stock. Rural. 2. A mistake or confusion, e.g., **to make a box of** (something), to muddle.

boxer: A bowler hat. Also, **bocker, bokker.** 2. The man who organises a two-up game, who arbitrates on all matters concerning bets laid and the tossing of the coins. Also called **centre man.** 3. A percentage, 10 to 20 per cent., of a **spinner's** winnings in two-up paid to the **ring-keeper** if the spinner heads the coins three times or more.

box-up, v.: To mix or confuse. See **box,** 2. As n., a confusion or muddle.

brass: A form of betting trick. Also v., to cheat or defraud.

break, v.: To cost, e.g., "What did that (object) **break you for?**" or "How much did it **break you?**" How much did it cost?

breakaway: A bullock that leaves a herd; a panic rush of cattle or sheep. Rural sl.

breakers, shoot the: To surf.

break it down! Be reasonable! Stop it! Also, **turn it up!**

breast, v.: To meet, accost, approach.

brick: A £10 note. See **sane.**

brickfielder: A heavy southerly wind in Sydney that carried dust and dirt into the central part of the town from nearby brickfields. Obs.

bridge: A fake bet laid to induce an observer to part with his money on a racecourse. 2. A form of approach, an introduction. 3. A plausible tale or excuse.

bridge, our: Sydney Harbour Bridge. Like **our 'arbour,** it is mainly used ironically by residents outside N.S.W.

brim: Aust. pronunciation for the word **bream,** the fish.

brinny: A stone.

Brissie: Brisbane.

brits up, have the: To be afraid or alarmed. Also, **to have the Jimmy Brit(t)s** and **have the jimmies.**

broad: A term applied to wool to signify that it is coarser or stronger in quality than is usual for that particular type of wool.

broke for: Short of, in need of (something), e.g., **broke for a feed,** hungry.

broken mouth: An old sheep. Rural sl.

bronzewing: A member of the proletariat. Rare. cf. **coppertail** and **silvertail.**

broomie: A boy who keeps a shearing shed floor swept of locks at shearing time. Rural sl.

brown bomber: A parking policeman in some cities.

brownie: A cake made like a damper with the addition of sugar, currants and fat. Also called **bush brownie.** Rural sl.

brumby: A wild horse.

brush: A girl or young woman.

brusher, give a: To go off without paying one's debts.

buck, v.: Used to describe the wild jumping and shying of an unbroken horse when ridden. Also, n.

buck, give it a: To make an attempt at (some task or undertaking); to try. Also **have a buck at.**

bucker: A horse that bucks.

bucking: The wild jumping and shying of an unbroken horse.

buckjump: To buck. Also to ride a bucking horse.

buckjumper: A horse that bucks; a person who rides a bucking horse.

Buckley's chance: No chance at all or a negligible chance of success. Whence, **haven't a Buckley's, haven't Buckley's, not a Buckley's;** also, **two chances, mine and Buckley's.**

budgie: Familiarism for the budgerigar, an Aust. bird.

bugle, on the: Unpleasant, worthless. Said of food (esp. meat) which is decaying. See **nose, on the.**

bull artist: A braggart, a teller of fanciful tales.

bull dust, bull fodder, bull's wool, bullsh: Nonsense, empty chatter, bragging.

bullo: Nonsense, empty talk.

bullock, v.: To do heavy manual work. Whence, **bullocking,** hard work.

bullocky: A driver of a team of bullocks or oxen. Whence, **bullock dray, bullock waggon, bullock whip.** Rare.

bullocky's joy: Treacle or golden syrup. Rare.

bull-puncher, bullock puncher: A cattle station hand or **ringer** (q.v.).

bullroarer: An aboriginal instrument used esp. in initiation ceremonies. It consists of a slab of wood or stone pierced at one end by a hole through which a string is passed. It is whirled round, making a noise supposed by natives to be the voice of a great spirit.

bumper: A cigarette end. Whence, **not worth a bumper,** worthless.

bumper-up: A pickpocket's confederate. Criminal sl.

bundle, drop your: See **drop your bundle.**

bung: See **bong.** 2. As in phrase **bung on an act,** to swear luridly, give way to temper, complain at length.

bung-eye: A painful eye inflammation caused by flies. Esp. rural sl.

bunk: As for **double-bank** (q.v.).

bunk off: To decamp, depart.

bunk-up, v.: To help (someone) to surmount an obstacle. As n., an act of assistance, esp. in climbing.

bunyip: A mythical and ill-disposed animal of aboriginal legend.

burl: An attempt at (some undertaking). Esp. **give it a burl,** to make an attempt, to take a chance.

burley: As for **berley.**

bush: Orig. applied (circa 1800) to scrub-covered or heavily wooded country. Whence, the country in general outside a capital; the suburbs of a city.

bush, go (of cattle or horses): To run wild. 2. (Of a person): To hide anywhere from scrutiny.

bush, take to the: Orig. to become a bushranger. Later, as for **go bush.**

bush, up the: In the backblocks, in inland country.

bush Baptist: A person of dubious religious persuasion or one who has no religious persuasion at all. Rare.

bush brother: A member of a **bush brotherhood** carrying on missionary work in the outback. **Bush Brotherhood Sunday** is observed in N.S.W. each October.

bush cake: See **cowyard cake.**

bush carpenter: A rough, handy carpenter.

bush dinner: Mutton, damper and milkless tea. Rare.

bushfire: Fire that occurs in a bush-covered area.

bushfire, full of: Full of vim or courage.

bush lawyer: A person who, with glib tongue and imagination, purports to solve legal problems and arguments among his fellows.

bushranger: Orig. an escaped convict who sought refuge in bush areas. Later, a bandit who operated in the country. Obs. Whence, any swindler or person who takes blatant advantage of others.

bush sickness: A form of stock sickness caused by lack of minerals in pastures.

bush scrubbers: Cattle that have gone bush and deteriorated in condition.

bush telegrams: Reports of police movements conveyed by word of mouth by confederates of bushrangers in country areas. Obs.

bush telegraph: A confederate of a bushranger who supplied news of police movements; general description of assorted sources of information about the police to reach bushrangers. Obs. 2. The supposed source of a rumour. Modern forms include **bush radio, bush wireless, bushwire, mulga wire.** cf. **Tom Collins.**

bushman's clock: A kookaburra.

bush up, v.: To confuse or bewilder (a person).

bush walk: A track in bushland; a long-distance hike through bush. Also, **bushwalker,** a person who hikes in the bush, often a member of a **bushwalking club.**

bushwhacker: A resident of the bush. Rare.

bust a rut: To blaze a trail.

buster: As for **southerly buster** (q.v.).

butcher: A small glass of beer. South Aust. sl. Equivalent to lady's waist or pony (q.v.) in N.S.W.

butchers: Angry. To be (go) butchers, to show anger.

butterfly: A coin that fails to spin when tossed in two-
up. cf. floater.

C

cabbage garden, cabbage patch: Victoria. Obs.

cabbage hat: As for next:

cabbage tree (hat): A low-crowned, broad-brimmed hat
made of fan-palm leaves, popular last century.
Whence, my cabbage tree! an exclamation; cabbage
tree mob, cabbageites, street toughs who favoured
the cabbage tree hat. Obs.

cacto: The insect cactoblastus, introduced into Aust. to
kill prickly pear. cf. myxo.

cake: A gold nugget. Obs. 2. A harlot. Whence, cake-
shop, brothel.

canary stain: A light yellow stain in wool that cannot be
scoured white; it occurs mainly in Q. and W.A.

carpet: A £1 note.

carrion: Cattle. Rural sl.

carry matilda: To hump a swag. cf. waltzing matilda.

carry the knot: As for above.

carry the mail: To stand drinks, to shout (q.v.).

cat, whip the: To cry over spilt milk.

catching pen: A pen in a woolshed from which a shearer
takes sheep to be shorn. Whence, catch, n., a sheep
taken by a shearer from his catching pen.

cattle duffer: A cattle thief. Whence, cattle duffing, the
stealing of cattle.

Centralia: The central Aust. area.

Centre, the: The central Aust. area.

centre man: See boxer, 2.

channel country: Regions in the north-east corner of
South Aust. and in the south-west corner of Q.,
stretching to the fringe of the Simpson Desert. In
wet periods, the many river courses fill and over-
flow, forming countless channels through the sand.

cheer chaser: One who curries favour, esp. one who seeks popular plaudits. Whence, **cheer chasing.**

cherry nose: A type of cicada.

chew someone's ear: To borrow money from a person. Also, **chew someone's lug.**

Chink: A Chinese.

chips: Split wood used as kindling for a fire.

Chloe, drunk as: Exceedingly drunk. Aust. synonyms include **drunk as a bastard, drunk as a fowl, drunk as a piss ant, drunk as an owl.**

chocolate soldier: A type of cicada.

chop: A wood-chopping contest for axemen.

chop-up, n.: A division of spoils.

Chow: A Chinese. Whence, **awkward as a Chow on a bike,** extremely awkward. 2. A term of contempt applied to a person—by rhyme with **cow** (q.v.).

chromo: A prostitute.

chronic: Over-persistent, excessive, extremely disagreeable.

chuck a charley: To throw a fit. Also, **chuck a sixer.**

chuck-in, n.: A voluntary subscription made by a number of persons, sometimes for the benefit of another, but more often to defray the costs of a celebration. The amount varies according to collective decision, i.e., **zack-in, deaner-in, two bob-in,** etc.

chuck off at: To sneer at, to chaff.

chutty: Chewing gum.

chyack, v.: To tease, jeer at.

city of churches: Adelaide.

clever: In good health, in good order, proficient. Used mainly in negative sense, **not too clever,** which often means extremely bad.

cliner, clinah: A sweetheart, a girl-friend. Obs.

clout, v.: To steal (something). Whence, **clout on,** to take, purloin.

coachers: Tame cattle used to decoy wild animals. Rural sl.

cobber: A friend, companion, workmate. Whence, **to cobber up with,** to become friends with (someone);

cobber-dobber, one who betrays a friend. See **dob in.**

cobbler: The last sheep in a shearing pen. Rural sl.

cock, hot: Nonsense, humbug. Also, a lot of cock.

cockatoo: A small farmer. cf. **cocky.** Also, **cockatooer, cockatoo selector, cockatoo settler.** Obs. 2. A look-out man, a **nitkeeper** (q.v.), one who keeps guard while illegal activity is afoot. Whence, **to cockatoo,** to act as a look-out man. cf. **keep nit.**

cockeye bob: A fierce thunderstorm or coastal cyclone, esp. in the far north. Also, **cockeyed bob.**

cocky: A farmer or outback settler, derived from **cockatoo** (q.v.). Whence, **cow cocky, scrub cocky, fruit cocky,** etc. Also, **boss cocky,** a leader, the head of a group. Derivatives worth noting include **cocky's clip,** a term used in shearing, "the equivalent of shaving a sheep"; **cocky's coal,** corncobs used as fuel for a fire; **cocky's crow,** dawn; **cocky's joy,** golden syrup; **cocky's string,** fencing wire. Now all rare. 2. A sheep which has lost some of its wool. Also, **parrot** and **rosella.**

colonial duck: Boned shoulder of mutton stuffed with sage and onions. Rare.

colonial goose: Boned leg of mutton stuffed with sage and onions. Rare.

combo: A white man who lives with an aboriginal female. Whence, **to combo** and **comboing.**

comeback: The progeny of a merino ram and a cross-bred ewe. See **Polwarth.**

come-on, the: A trickster's inducement to his victim.

commo: A Communist.

compo: Workers' Compensation. **On the compo,** in receipt of workers' compensation; **compo king,** a man who exploits the benefits of workers' compensation.

concertina: A side of mutton or lamb. 2. A sheep that is hard to shear because of the wrinkles in its skin. Rural sl.

Congo: A Congregationalist.

cooee: A penetrating cry, used esp. in bush country. Also, **to cooee,** to use such a cry to attract attention; **within cooee,** within calling distance, close at hand.

coolamon: An aboriginal wooden vessel for carrying food, etc.

Coolgardie safe: A rough wood and sacking foodbin which serves as a crude refrigerator in the outback. The stress is on **cool** rather than on the place-name, **Coolgardie.**

coppertail: A member of the proletariat.

corella: A sheep with patches of wool hanging loose. Rural sl. See **cocky,** 2.

corner: A share, esp. a share of plunder. Criminal sl.

Corner, the: The junction of the north-eastern point of the South Aust. boundary and Qld. Whence, **corner country.**

Cornstalk: An Australian. Obs.

Corriedale: A breed of sheep first evolved in Otago, N.Z., in the 1860s.

corroboree: An aboriginal ceremonial dance, usually with chanting. 2. A social gathering, a public meeting, a disturbance or noise (made by people).

corroboree water: Cheap wine.

cossie: A swimming costume.

couldn't do it in the time! he (you): Sarcastic comment addressed to a person who threatens to fight, but who has little chance of success.

coupla: Several drinks, but not necessarily two. 2. Two coins which fall "heads" when tossed.

cow: An unpleasant person or event. Sometimes used as genial reference to a person. See **fair cow.**

cowyard cake: A cake or bun containing a few sultanas. Also, **bush cake.** Rural sl.

cowyard confetti: Nonsense, empty chatter. As for **bull dust, meadow mayonnaise,** etc.

crack down on: To seize, to make off with. Also, to curb, as in **crack down on someone,** take a person to task.

crack hardy: To put on a courageous front in response to misfortune.

crack it: To record success in an amorous exploit.

cracker: A £1 note.

cray: A crayfish.

creamy: A quarter-caste aboriginal girl.

crimp: The "wave" in wool fibre, a visible indication of its character and quality. The smaller and more even the crimp usually the finer the wool.

cronk: Dishonest, worthless, out-of-order.

crook: Ill, out-of-sorts, esp. **to be crook, to feel crook.** 2. Angry, annoyed; esp. **to go crook,** to express displeasure; **to go crook at** (someone), to vent one's anger on someone. 3. Spurious, worthless.

crooked on: Ill-disposed towards. See **crook, 2.**

croweater: A South Australian.

cruel, v.: To spoil or ruin (something), e.g., a person's chances of success.

crumb act, put on the: To impose on another person; to **bludge** (q.v.).

crutch, stiff as a: Broke, penniless, extremely unfortunate.

cundy: A small stone.

Cunnamulla cartwheel: A big, broad-brimmed hat. Obs.

cunning up on yourself: Being so smart that one creates pitfalls for oneself; to be hoist with one's own petard.

Cup, the: The Melbourne Cup race or meeting.

curl the mo, to: To succeed, to win outstandingly. cf. **big twist.**

currency: An old term used to describe a person born in Aust. in contrast to **sterling,** applied to a Briton. Whence, **currency lad, currency lass.** All obs.

curry, to give: To abuse (someone); to express anger at a person.

curse: A tramp's swag or bluey. Whence, **carry (or hump) the curse.** Rare.

custards: Pimples.

cut: A job as a shearer, e.g., **get a cut** (at a station). Also, **cut-out,** the completion of shearing on a station. Rural sl.

cut out, v.: To separate cattle or other stock from a herd or mob. 2. To complete shearing at a shed. 3. To complete any task.

D

Dad and Dave: Two fictional characters, created by Steele Rudd in the 1890s and since elaborated on stage, screen and radio as typifying raw, outback humour.

dag: An amusing or odd person. Whence, **dag,** adj., good, excellent; **a dag at,** expert at.

damper: Bread baked in the ashes of a fire.

Darlo: The district of Darlinghurst, Sydney.

dart: A scheme, plan, dodge; a desirable object. Rare.

Dart, the Old: England.

dead as mutton: Dead, obsolete, out of fashion.

deadbeat: A man down on his luck or without money. Also, **deadbroker.**

dead bird: A certainty.

dead-copper: A police informer.

dead hand: An expert.

Dead Heart, the: The remote desert areas of inland Aust.

dead lair: See **lair.**

dead nuts on: Opposed to, antagonistic towards.

dead ring of: Exactly or strikingly similar to. Also, **dead spotted ling of,** rhyming sl. influenced by **dead spit of,** both used in the same way.

deadwood fence: A rough rural fence built of fallen branches and logs. Rural sl. Rare.

death-adders in one's pocket, to have: To be mean with money.

deaner, deener: A shilling.

demon: A policeman, a detective.

derry on: A suspicion or grudge against a person. Also, **to derry,** to dislike.

devil devil: Rough country broken up with holes and hillocks. Rural sl.

devil-on-the-coals: A small type of **damper** (q.v.). Obs.

dice, v.: To reject, throw away.

dickin! Cut it out! Be reasonable! Also, **dickin on it!**

didjeridu: An aboriginal musical instrument, varying in size from a foot or so long to 8 ft. The music is a nasal whine amplified by the hollow tube of the instrument.

die on it: To let someone down; to fail to keep a promise.

diggings: A non-alluvial goldfield; goldfields in general. Obs.

digger: Orig. a gold miner. 2. An Aust. soldier.

dill: A simpleton or fool. Whence, **dilpot** or **dillpot**. 2. A trickster's victim. Criminal sl.

dilly: Silly, by rhyme. See **dill**, 1.

dillybag: A small bag used for general carrying purposes. Orig. an aboriginal's string bag.

ding: An Italian.

dingo: A betrayer, cheat, sneak. Whence, **to dingo on**, to betray, let down (someone).

dingy (of wool): Thin, discoloured and wasty wool that may not scour white.

dink: A Chinese, by rhyme on **Chink**.

dink, v.: See **double-dink**.

dinkum: True, vouched for, honest. Whence, **fair dinkum** and **square dinkum**.

dinkum Aussie: A born-Australian; an Aust. patriot. Also, **dinkydie Aussie**.

dinkum oil: Truth, inside information of strict authenticity. Also, **dinkum article**.

dinkydie, adj.: True, honest, fully reliable.

dip: A swim in either fresh or salt water. 2. A simpleton or fool.

dirt, put in the: To play foul in any game or contest; to act unfairly; to make unnecessary trouble. Also, **do dirt on** and **play the dirty**.

dirty big: Extremely large.

do a perish: Almost to die for want of a drink. Mainly outback in use. Also, **a perishing track**, a route lacking water.

do one's block: See **block, do one's**.

do some good for yourself: To record success in an amorous exploit. (Mainly a masculine phrase; cf. **crack it.**)

dob in, v.: To betray, to focus blame on another; esp. **to dob someone in.** Whence, **cobber-dobber.** See **cobber.**

dodger: Food of any kind. Whence, **yunk of dodger,** a slice of bread.

doer: An amusing or odd person. Esp. **hard doer** and **good doer.**

dog: Food. Rural sl. A reference to the dog that sat on a tucker-box near Gundagai. See **tucker.** 2. A plainclothes railway detective. 3. A drinking debt. See **dog, tie up a.**

doggy (of wool): Straight in fibre, lacking what woolclassers call "breeding," with little felting property.

dog licence: A Certificate of Exemption to allow an aboriginal to buy drink in a hotel.

dog, tie up a: To book up drinks in a hotel bar.

dog-list, on the: To be barred from drinking in a hotel.

dog's breakfast: A confusion, mess, turmoil.

Domain dosser: A loafer or down-and-out frequenting the Sydney Domain. Also, **Domain squatter.**

donah, doner: A sweetheart, girl-friend. Obs.

don't do anything you couldn't eat! Don't bite off more than you can chew. A warning to a boastful or pugnacious person.

don't wake it up! Don't talk about it! Let sleeping dogs lie!

double-bank: See next:

double-dink, v.: To carry a second person on a horse or on the top bar of a bicycle. As n., the practice of so transporting a person. Exchangeable terms are **dink, donk** and **double-bank,** both as v. and n.

double drummer: A type of cicada.

double fleece: The fleece of a sheep which has missed one shearing and has been brought in for the next clip. Whence, **double-fleecer,** such a sheep.

double-dump: See **dump.**

dover: A clasp knife. Rare.

down, n.: A grudge against a person; an objection against something. Whence, **a down on** and **have a down on.**

down on, get: To steal, remove, appropriate.

drack (of a woman): Unattractive, unworthy of male attention. Esp. **drack sort.** See **sort.**

draft on the camp: To cut out (q.v.) cattle.

drag on, v. (of a man): To marry, i.e., **drag on a woman.** 2. To undertake. cf. **pull on.**

drag the chain: To be slow, to lag behind in work or other activity.

dreaming: An aboriginal totemic site; a place which a totemic ancestor inhabits; a totem, e.g., **emu dreaming, fly dreaming.**

dream time: The aboriginal concept of Creation, "in the beginning."

drink with the flies: To drink alone; a drink taken alone. cf. **Jimmy Woodser.**

drongo: A simpleton, fool, **no-hoper** (q.v.).

drop, v.: To strike, knock out. Esp. as threat, **I'll drop you! (yer!)**

drop one's bundle: To panic, to give up trying.

drop the bucket: To throw responsibility for an offence on to someone else. Criminal sl.

drover's guide: As for **bagman's gazette** (q.v.).

drum: A swagman's rolled blanket and the belongings placed within it. cf. **bluey.**

drum, the: The true facts, sound advice; a valuable tip. Esp. **give someone the drum.** Also, v., **to drum,** to inform; to advise; to explain the correct facts.

drunk as a fowl: Very drunk. A rhyming variant of the older **drunk as an owl.**

drunk-up: A drinking bout or drunken party.

dry, the: The winter and generally rainless season in Aust.'s far north. 2. Waterless country or desert.

dry as a sunstruck bone: Extremely dry; drought-stricken. Also, **to dry up like a sunstruck billabong.** Both similes are also used figuratively: "dry" suggest-

ing irony, and "dry-up" meaning to become silent
or run out of words.

dry old stick: Genial reference to an elderly person.

duckhouse, up against one's: A phrase used to describe
some setback to a person's plans, e.g., **that's one up
against your duckhouse!** That baffles you! That
makes you think!

dud up: Deliberately to misinform or mislead (someone).
Whence, **dudder** and **dudder-upper.** Criminal sl.

duff, v.: To steal cattle or horses, esp. in large numbers.
Whence, **duffer** and **duffing.**

dump, n.: A small silver coin worth 1/3 used in Aust.
between 1813 and 1829. It was punched from the
centre of a silver dollar; the remainder of the coin
was known as a **ring dollar** or **holey dollar.** Obs.
2. A cache of stolen goods. 3. Any place, residence,
lodging or office.

dump, v.: To press wool in a bale. Also, **double-dump,**
v., to press two bales of wool together for carriage;
as n., two bales of wool so pressed together.

dumper: A heavy wave that, unlike an ordinary breaker
in the Aust. surf, collapses suddenly and with great
force. Whence, **to be dumped,** to be caught by such
a wave. 2. A cigarette end. Whence, **dumper-
dasher,** a collector of cigarette ends in the street.
cf. **bumper.**

dungaree settler: An outback settler of the poorest financial resources. Obs.

dust: Flour. Rural sl.

dwell on: To follow or watch (a person) closely; eagerly
to await another's decision or action.

dynamite: Baking powder. Mainly rural sl.

E

eaglehawk, v.: To pluck wool from a dead sheep.
Whence, **eaglehawking,** the practice.

ear, on one's: Drunk. 2. (Of a task or undertaking)
easily accomplished.

earlies, the: The early days in Aust. settlement.

earlugger: A borrower.

early risers: Thin blankets carried by swagmen. Rare.

Eastralia: The eastern States of Aust. cf. **Centralia, Westralia.**

easy: Moderately disposed towards (esp. towards some proposal by another person); indifferent whether a decision is made for or against. Esp. **to be easy,** not to care which way a decision goes.

edge against, have an: To dislike (a person).

edge, over the: Unreasonable; beyond the limits of commonsense, decency or justice.

eeler-spee: A trickster or **spieler** (q.v.). Criminal sl.

endless belt: A prostitute.

Enzed: New Zealand. Whence, **Enzedder,** a New Zealander.

even terms: Working for one's food. Rural sl.

evo: Evening. See **arvo.**

Ex., his: His Excellency, applied to a Governor-General or State Governor.

eyepicker: One who **picked the eyes out of** a grazing district by taking up the best land. See **peacock.** Obs.

eyes out: With maximum effort. Esp. **go eyes out,** work hard, travel rapidly.

extra grouse: Extra well or attractive; (something) meriting great approval. cf. **grouse.**

F

fadge: A butt of a bale of wool or two bags sewn together, usual weight 60 lb. to 150 lb. (A full bale of greasy wool usually weighs around 300 lb.)

fair cow: An exceedingly unpleasant person, situation or turn of events. cf. **cow.**

fair crack of the whip: Said of fair dealing. Esp. **give someone (or have) a fair crack of the whip.**

fair dinkum: Honest, true, genuine. Also, **square dinkum.** cf. **dinkum.**

fair enough! A general expression of approval or acquiescence.

fair go! Be reasonable!

fangs in, put the: To borrow money from (a person). Also, **put the nips in, bite** and **sting.**

fat as a match: Extremely thin.

fat cake: A small fried cake of flour. Rural sl. Rare.

fatty: Synonym for **brownie** (q.v.).

feather bedding: An industrial term used in reference to overloading a gang on a wharf so that one member, usually an elderly wharfie, can earn money without doing a fair share of the work.

fed with: Tired of, bored with.

fence, over the: Unreasonable, unfair. cf. **edge, over the.**

fencing wire, tough as: Extremely tough or hardy.

ferry: A prostitute.

fiddlearse about: To waste time, "mess around."

fiddley: A £1 note. Also, **fiddleydid,** a rhyme on "quid."

finalise: To complete. Whence, **finalisation.**

financial: In funds, with ready money available. Whence, **to be financial.** cf. **holding.**

finger out! pull your: Hurry up!

First Fleet: The ships which brought the orig. convicts and their keepers to Aust. in 1788. Whence, **First Fleeter. Second Fleet** and **Third Fleet** also receive occasional literary reference.

first-up: For the first time; on the first occasion of endeavour.

Fitzroy Yank: An Aust. male, esp. a youth, who is trying to pass himself off as an American. Melbourne sl. cf. **Pyrmont Yank** and **Woolloomooloo Yank.**

fix the old gumtree, v. (used in reference to a wanderer): To settle down. Rural sl. Rare.

fixing: Strong drink.

fizgig: A police informer. Sometimes spelt **phizgig.** See **gig.**

fizz: As for **fizgig.**

fizz-out: A person on whom no reliability can be placed. **To fizz out on,** to let down, to fail in a promise.

flag: A banknote, esp. a £1 note.

flash: Ostentatious in dress and/or manner; (of a horse) high-spirited as in the idiomatic phrase, **flash as a Chinky's horse.**

flatite: A flat dweller.

flat out like a lizard: Ideas of lying flatly (on one's face, not one's back) and of travelling or working at great speed are recorded in the phrases **flat out like a lizard drinking** and **flat out like a lizard on a log.**

fleecepicker, fleecy: A woolshed hand detailed to pick up shorn fleeces. Rural sl.

Flemington confetti: Rubbish, nonsense, "bullsh." Mainly Sydney sl.

Flemo: Flemington racecourse and district, Melbourne. cf. **Darlo, Paddo, Kenso.**

flies about, no: Alert, wide awake; a phrase in which recognition is made of the shrewdness or sharp wit of someone.

floater: A penny that fails to spin when tossed in two-up. cf. **butterfly.**

flossy up: To dress up, to make oneself tidy; to improve one's appearance or the appearance of any object or possession. cf. **lair up.**

floury baker: A type of cicada.

fluff, v.: To break wind.

fly, n.: An attempt at (something), e.g., **give it a fly, have a fly at.**

flyblown: Penniless.

flybog: Jam.

fly country: Hot back-country in Aust.

flyjerks: Small pieces of cork suspended from the brim of a swagman's hat to ward off flies. Obs.

flystrike: Infestation of sheep by blowflies. Whence, **fly-struck.** Also, **body-strike.**

fly-swisher stew: Oxtail stew.

food inspector: A swagman. Obs.

footback, on: On foot.

force, n.: The ability of a sheepdog to control a mob of sheep, esp. without **legging,** i.e., leg-biting. A good dog is said to have a lot of force. Whence, **forcing dog.** See **huntaway.**

fortie: A crook or sharper.

fossick, v.: To search for surface gold. 2. To rummage about for something. Often, **fossick about** or **fossick around.** Also, **fossick up, fossicker,** and **fossicking.**

fowlhouse, up against one's: As for **duckhouse, up against one's.** Rare.

frames: Draft cattle. Rural sl.

Freddy, blind: See **blind Freddy.**

free select, v.: To take up Government land as a **free selector.** Obs. Also, **free selection** and **free selecting.**

freeze, do a: To be overlooked or ignored.

freezer: A sheep bred for export.

Fremantle doctor: A refreshing sea-breeze that blows into Fremantle and Perth after a hot day.

fribby (of wool): Containing an excessive amount of what are called **second cuts** and **sweat points,** i.e., inferior wool.

frig-up: A confusion or muddle.

frill, v.: Partly to ring-bark a tree. Rural sl.

frog: A £1 note. Also, **frogskin.**

front, v.: To mask the operations of a pickpocket accomplice. cf. **bumper-up.** Criminal sl.

frosty face: A defect sometimes occurring in merinos, characterised by chalky, harsh, white hairs covering the face. Rural sl.

fryingpan brand: A large brand used by cattle thieves to cover the rightful owner's brand. Rural sl.

full as a goog: Extremely drunk. See **goog.** Also, **full as a boot, full as an egg, full as a tick.**

full-mouth: An eight-tooth sheep. The terms **failing-mouth, gummy, broken-mouth** and **chisel-mouth** describe aged sheep.

full quid: In full possession of one's faculties. A person who is said to be **ten bob in the quid** or any smaller sum down to **tuppence in the quid,** is held to be stupid.

furphy: A rumour, a canard. Whence, **furphy king,** a specialist in spreading rumours. cf. **Tom Collins.**

G

galah: A fool, a crass idiot. (Pronounced ga-LAH.)

game as Ned Kelly: Highly courageous; willing to tackle big odds. Synonymous similes are **game as a pebble** and **game as a piss ant.**

garbo: A garbage collector.

gastro: The sickness known as gastroenteritis.

gay: A trickster's victim. Criminal sl.

geebung: An old settler. Obs.

get down on: To steal, "souvenir."

get on someone's works: To annoy, infuriate a person.

get someone set: To have a grudge against a person; to prepare to pay someone out.

get stuck into: To abuse (someone) verbally; to fight; to tackle a task energetically.

get the run: To be dismissed from a job.

get the spear: As for **get the run.**

getting any? This expression needs some explanation. It is usually addressed by man to man and enquires whether the listener has been achieving amorous successes of late. The formulas of reply include: **Climbing trees to get away from it! Got to swim under water to dodge it!** and **So busy I've had to put a man on!**

get tonked: To be struck or beaten in a fight. Also **get stoushed.**

get wet: To lose one's temper.

Ghan, the: The train that runs from Adelaide to Alice Springs.

gibber: A boulder or stone. Whence, **gibber country, gibber plain,** an inland area covered with stones. (The g is pronounced as in **go.**)

gig, n.: An observer; one who stares curiously. Whence, **to gig (at),** to stare. 2. A detective. 3. A simpleton or fool.

gig, v.: To toss coins in two-up so that they do not spin. cf. **butterfly** and **floater.**

gigglesuit: Prison garb. Criminal sl.

gin: An aboriginal woman. Whence, **gin jockey,** a white man who cohabits with an aboriginal woman. cf. **combo.** 2. Any married woman. 3. A saddle.

ging: A child's catapult. cf. **shot-ging.**

ginger: A harlot who works with another girl (sometimes with a man) to rob a client. Also, **ginger girl** and **gingerer.** Whence, **gingering,** the practice.

gip artist: A professional rogue, confidence trickster.

give away: To reject or abandon.

give best: To acknowledge defeat or the superiority of another.

give the game away: To abandon interest in any activity or pursuit.

go, n.: An agreement, a settled decision, e.g., **it's a go,** that's agreed on. 2. An iguana or goanna.

goanna: A piano.

goat: Like the **bandicoot** (q.v.), this animal has acquired a considerable place in Aust. idiom, e.g., **act the angora, rough as goat's knees, hard as goat's knees, run like a hairy goat, more kid in him than a goat in the family way.**

go for the doctor: To bet everything available on a race-horse in the expectation of making big money.

go lemony at: To become angry, express anger at (someone). cf. **crook, 2.**

go mulga: To decamp, take to the bush. See **bush, go.**

go off: When a hotel or club is raided by police for permitting after-hours drinking or gambling, it is said to **go off.** 2. When a horse or greyhound is "fixed" to win a race, it is said to **go off.**

go through: See **shoot through.**

go through without the waterbag (of a swagman or bush traveller): To be in a great hurry. Obs.

gog-eye: A child's catapult. cf. **ging, shanghai.**

gollion: A gob of phlegm. Also, **golly.** See **goo, v.**

gone to Moscow: Pawned. See **Moscow.**

goo, v.: To spit out a gob of phlegm. Also, **to goob.**

good! The use of this word as a formula of enigmatic reply merits mention. Esp. used by children, its senses embrace everything from passable to excellent, e.g., "How are you?"–"Good!" "How's work?"–"Good!" "How's school?" – "Good!" "How's your family?"–"Good!"

good doer: As for **doer** (q.v.).

good ink: (Something) pleasant, desired. Also, **good iron.**

good oil: Correct information, an accurate tip. See **dinkum oil.**

good on you! A general term of approval, but sometimes used ironically.

good sort: A girl or young woman, esp. one likely to yield to masculine ardour. See **sort.**

goodoh! A general term of approval with senses ranging from Excellent! Yes! and All right! to Perhaps!

gooey: A gob of phlegm. See **goo, v.**

goog: An egg. Whence, **full as a goog,** drunk; also well-fed.

googly: A ball in cricket which breaks from the off, although apparently bowled as a leg-break. 2. An awkward question which a person would rather not answer.

gooly: A pebble or stone.

government house: The homestead of a head station. Rural sl.

government stroke, the: A lazy method of working.

graft: Any form of work, but esp. hard work. Also, **to graft,** to work hard; **grafter,** a hard worker; **grafting,** hard work.

grease, in the (of wool): Raw wool containing its natural yolk. Also, **greasy wool.**

greengrocer: A type of cicada.

green monday: A type of cicada. See **yellow monday, yellow tuesday, black friday:** these allusions to days of the week are based on an old error. cf. **yellow monday.**

griff, the: True information; a correct tip.

groper: A Western Australian. Also, **sandgroper.** Whence, **groperland,** Western Aust.

group: This industrial and political term refers to industrial groups which were formed in 1945 by the A.L.P. to combat Communism in Australian trade unions. They were subsequently disbanded on the ground that they had become instruments for infiltration by Catholic Action. See next:

groupers: Those who advocate the re-formation of **groups** (see above) or who support the principle of fighting Communism by means of the **groups** are known as **groupers.** In the late 1950s, the term was used by left-wingers to describe those who still operate within the Australian Labour Party under the influence of Catholic Action.

grouse: Good, excellent.

grouter: A bet in two-up (q.v.) laid on tails after a long run of heads or vice versa. Whence, **grouter bet** and **come in on the grouter.** 2. An advantage, esp. an unfair advantage.

guiver: See **guyver.**

gulf country: Country in the Gulf of Carpentaria area in North Queensland.

gully: Any geographical indentation from a fair-sized drain to a vast valley.

gullyraker: A cattle thief. 2. A long cattle whip.

gumleaf band: A group of (usually aboriginal) musicians who make music by blowing on gumtree leaves. Also, **gumleaf player.**

gumleaves growing out of the ears, to have: A phrase descriptive of someone, esp. a simple-minded person, who has lived long in the bush or outback.

gummy (of scoured wool): Containing a large quantity of yolk or lanolin. As n., a sheep which is toothless with age.

gumsucker: A Victorian; whence, an Aust. Both obs.

gumtree, to have seen one's last: To be on the verge of death. Rural sl.

gumtree, up a: In trouble, in a quandary. cf. **up a wattle.**

gun: An expert shearer.

gunyah: A humpy (q.v.) or shack.

gutter: The space in front of a racecourse totalisator.

guyver: Affectation, make-believe, "side," spurious talk.

H

had it, to have: To have been killed, destroyed, consumed, rendered ineffectual. This expression found wide application in World War II.

hairy goat, run like a (used esp. of racehorses): To perform badly in a race.

halfbred sheep: Orig. a sheep by a longwool ram from a merino ewe; now loosely applied to the type. Corriedale sheep were orig. called **in-bred half-breeds;** "now in-bred half-bred flocks are those which re-introduce merino or longwool blood, while the Corriedale flocks can only introduce Corriedale blood."

half-cut: Silly, stupid; drunk.

half-pie: Worthless.

half-rinsed: Drunk.

half-squarie: A prostitute.

hang up a horse: To hitch a horse to a post. Rural sl.

happy as Larry: Extremely happy or contented.

hard case: An amusing or eccentric person; a daredevil. Also, **hard doer.**

hard hitter: A bowler hat.

hard word on, put the: To ask (someone) for a loan. 2. Used esp. for a masculine request to a woman for her favours.

haste! Look out! Mainly used in criminal jargon. Whence, **haste it!** to cease some activity, equivalent of Stop it! Synonymous is **ace it!**

hatful of worms, silly as a: Extremely silly or stupid. Also, **silly as a bag of worms.**

hatracks: Thin or scrawny cattle or horses. Mainly rural sl.

hatter: A person who lives alone, esp. in the outback. 2. A lone criminal. **Hatting,** living on one's own.

haven't (hasn't) Buckley's: Used in reference to a person who has little or no chance of success. See **Buckley's.**

haven't (hasn't) the bolter's: As for above.

Hawkesburies: The shivers or shakes. Truncated from rhyming sl. **Hawkesbury rivers,** shivers.

head: A professional two-up gambler. 2. A long-sentence prisoner. Criminal sl.

heads on 'em like mice: A phrase used to express awe at any strong combination.

head them: To play **two-up** (q.v.). Often, **head 'em.**

Heart, the: The central areas of Aust. From **Dead Heart** (q.v.).

heifer dust: Nonsense, "bullsh." cf. **meadow mayonnaise, cowyard confetti,** etc.

hive off: To depart.

hock: A homosexual male.

hoist, v.: To strike (someone) with the fist. 2. To steal, "souvenir."

hold, v.: To be in funds; to be **financial** (q.v.).

hold your horses! Hold on! Not so fast!

holding: In funds. See **hold, v.**

hole: A pool, **billabong** (q.v.). Esp. in forms **swimming hole, water hole.**

holey dollar: A large silver coin out of which a **dump** (q.v.) was punched. Obs. Also **holy dollar.**

home on the pig's back: Easily completed. Applied to any activity that requires little effort or ingenuity to finish.

Home: Britain. Orig. used affectionately, now often used ironically. See **homey.**

homey: A Briton; a migrant from **Home** (q.v.).

honeypot: A method of jumping into water with the hands clasped round the knees. Children's sl.

honest to dinkum: True, vouched for. See **dinkum.**

honk, v.: To stink. Also, **honk like a gaggle of geese.** cf. **hoot.**

hook one's bait: To depart.

hooray! Goodbye!

hooroo! Goodbye!

hoot: Money, ready cash.

hoot, v.: To stink. cf. **honk.**

hop: A policeman. See **john hop.**

hop into: To attack, make short work of (a person or task).

hospital sheep: Sick sheep that are placed alone. Rural sl.

hostile: Angry, annoyed. Whence, **go hostile** and **go hostile at,** express anger or annoyance (at a person).

hot: Well (in health), good, proficient at. Often used negatively, **not so hot,** not feeling well or not achieving much. 2. Excessive, unreasonable. 3. Stinking. cf. **hoot.**

hot cack: Good, excellent.

hottie: A tall, rather than a dubious or "hot" story.

Hoyts, the man outside: A mythical person alleged to create rumours. cf. **Tom Collins** and **furphy.**

hum: To borrow, scrounge.

hummer: A borrower, a scrounger.

hump, v.: To shoulder or carry. Used esp. in **hump a bluey (drum** or **curse).**

humpy: Any small hut or shack.

hungerfine: An ultrafine type of wool caused by starvation.

hungry: Selfish, mean.

huntaway: A sheepdog which drives sheep forward when mustering. Also called a **forcing dog.** See **force.**

hurrah, on the: A boss or ganger shouting at and rushing his men is said to work **on the hurrah.**

hut-keep, v.: To look after a hut or living quarters in the bush or on a station. Whence, **hut-keeper, hut-keeping.** Rural sl.

I

identity, old: An old, noted inhabitant of a locality. Often, **an identity,** with the word "old" omitted.

illywacker: A trickster or spieler. Criminal sl.

imbo: A trickster's victim. Criminal sl.

improve, on the: Improving in health or proficiency.

in the blue: Out of control.

in the book: As used in "He's in the book, but he doesn't know what page he's on!" He's all right, but he's not very smart.

in the wool (of sheep): Ready or nearly ready for shearing. Rural sl.

in smoke: In hiding.

info: Information.

inked: Drunk.

inland: Any part of the Aust. mainland that is not on the coast; specifically, the outback or remote central areas of the continent. Whence, **inlander.** cf. **inside country.**

inside country: Well-populated country near or in coastal areas, specifically in contrast to **inland** or **outback.**

inside squatter: A farmer or large land-owner in a fairly well-populated district.

ironbark, adj.: Strong, unyielding.

iron man: A £1 note.

issue, the: Everything, the lot.

it's a gig! It's extremely good.

J

jack: A policeman, a detective. 2. Familiar nickname for a kookaburra; abbreviated from **jackass** and **laughing jackass.** 3. A double-headed penny.

jack of: Tired of, fed up with. Whence, **jack the contract,** to leave a job.

jack shay: A tin quart pot used for boiling water or cooking in the bush or outback. Rural sl.

Jack Smithers: A lone drink or a lone drinker. Obs. See **Jimmy Woodser.**

Jack the painter: Strong bush tea. Rural sl. Obs.

jackeroo: A station hand who is being trained for managerial status. Also, v., **to jackeroo,** to work in such capacity; **jackerooing,** such work.

jacko: A kookaburra. See **jack, 2.**

Jack Rice couldn't jump over, a roll: Considerable ready money; a large roll of banknotes. Also, **a roll that would choke an anteater, a roll big enough to choke a bullock, a wad that would choke a wombat.**

Jacky: An aboriginal male. Whence, **sit up like Jacky,** to sit up straight and behave with restraint.

Jacky Howe: A short-sleeved shirt favoured by shearers.

jacky raw: A new chum. Obs.

jagging, go: To make a social visit, usually with the aim of gossiping.

jamberoo: A lively (esp. a drunken) party. cf. **shivoo.**

jar: A pint of beer.

jarrah-jerker: A timber-getter in Western Aust.

jerry, v.: To understand, realise, "tumble to."

jewey: A jewfish; a jew lizard. Also, **jewie, jewy.**

jim: The sum of £1.

jimmy: An immigrant (rhyming sl.), a new chum. Obs. Also, **jimmy grant.** See **pommy.**

Jimmy Woodser: A solitary drink; **a drink with the flies.** Also, a solitary drinker.

jinker: A large conveyance with four wheels for transporting logs. cf. **junker.**

job, v.: To hit with the fist.

joe! joe-joe! joey! Cries of warning once widely used on goldfields to notify the approach of troopers. Obs.

joe: A police trooper. Obs. 2. A penny. 3. A snake, from rhyming sl. **Joe Blake.**

joes: Melancholy feelings, the "blues."

joey: A baby kangaroo, also the young of other marsupials. 2. A young child. 3. A minor lie or evasion. 4. A threepenny bit. 5. Something worthless. Criminal sl. 6. A fraud. Criminal sl.

joey, wood and water: A handyman on a station homestead.

john: A policeman; from **john hop.** cf. **jack.** 2. A Chinese. Also, **John Chinaman.**

john hop: A policeman. Also, **jonnop, johndarm.**

johnny cake: A small **damper** (q.v.) baked in the embers of a fire. Rural sl.

Johnny Warder: A lone drinker. Obs. like **Jack Smithers.** Both were former alternatives to **Jimmy Woodser** (q.v.).

jollop: Strong liquor.

jonah, v.: To ruin, hinder, "jinx," bring misfortune.

jonnick: Right, correct, honest. Obs.

jumbuck: A sheep.

jump-out, the: The beginning (of some activity).

jump-up: A mixture of flour and water boiled into a paste with sugar. Rural sl. Rare. 2. A sudden rise in country encountered on an outback journey. Rural sl.

junker: As for **jinker.**

just quietly: Confidentially; between you and me.

K

kangaroo: A native of Aust.; an Aust.-born person. Obs. 2. A representative Aust. footballer. 3. A prison warder, by rhyme on "screw." Also abbreviated to **kanga.** Criminal sl.

kangaroo fence: A fence constructed of rough logs placed upright close together. Rural sl. Obs.

kangarooland: Australia. Obs.

kangarooer: A person who hunts kangaroos. Whence, **kangarooing.**

kangaroos in one's top paddock, to have: To be silly, crazy.

keep a dog and bark yourself? why: A self-explanatory sentence.

keep down: To retain (esp. a job), to hold against any competition.

keep nit: To mount guard, keep watch, esp. while some illegal activity is afoot. cf. **nitkeeper** and **cockatoo, 2.**

keep out of the rain: To avoid trouble.

keep your end up: To do your bit in any joint activity.

kelly: A crow. 2. An axe. Whence, **on the kelly,** engaged in axe work.

Kelly, Ned: Any person of buccaneering business habits.

Kelly gang: Any group of people who make ruthless financial demands.

kelpie: A widely used type of sheepdog.

Kennedy rot: Land scurvy. Obs.

Kenso: Kensington racecourse and/or district. cf. **Darlo, Paddo.** All mainly Sydney sl.

key: The Habitual Criminals Act, 1905, or detention under this Act, e.g., "He's doing a swy (two years) and a **key,**" "He's done his spin (five years) and he's into his **key** now." Whence, **key-man,** a prisoner held under this Act. Criminal sl.

kia ora! Goodbye! So long! (From N.Z.)

kick: Pocket.

kick off: To die.

Kidman's blood mixture: Treacle. Rural sl. Obs. Also, **Kidman's joy.**

kidney-pie: Flattery, as for next.

kidstakes: Pretence, nonsense. Esp. in phrase **cut the kidstakes!** stop your nonsense! stop beating round the bush!

kill a snake: Equivalent of "to see a man about a dog." Rural sl.

killer: The straw that breaks the camel's back; the final action or argument which means the end to whatever hopes have been held. 2. A sheep designed for mutton. Rural sl.

king dick: A boss, leader.

king hit: A knock-out blow, esp. when its recipient is unprepared for it. 2. A person using such a blow. Also, **king-hit artist, king-hit merchant.**

kip: A narrow strip of wood, wide enough and long enough to accommodate two pennies, used in tossing these coins in two-up.

kiss the cross: To be knocked out in a fight.

kiwi: A New Zealander.

knife-edge: A sand-dune ridge in the desert. Rural sl.

knob: A double-headed penny.

knock, v.: To criticise unfavourably. Whence, **knocker,** such a critic; **knocking,** the practice. 2. To consume a drink, esp. **knock back** or **knock over**. 3. To rape. Criminal sl.

knock-back: A rebuff, disappointment.

knock-down: A formal introduction.

knocker: A persistently unfavourable critic. 2. A bookmaker who welshes on his clients. Whence, **to take the knock on,** to welsh.

knock out, v.: To earn (a sum of money).

knock rotten: To trounce, defeat thoroughly.

knuckle, close to the: Vulgar, indecent.

knuckle on, go the: To cheat, defraud, take down.

kurl: As for **curl** in **curl the mo** (q.v.).

L

lady's waist: A 5 oz. glass of beer. Also, **pony.** N.S.W. sl.

lair: A flashily dressed and uncouthly mannered young man. Whence, **dead lair** or **mug lair,** a particularly obnoxious **lair.** All used as general terms of opprobrium.

lairise, v.: To dress or act as a **lair.**

lair up, v.: To dress up, esp. to don one's best clothes for a festive occasion.

lairy: Vulgar in manners, flashily dressed. See **lair.**

lamb-down, v. (of station workers): To spend money lavishly on drink. Also (for a publican), to encourage such spending. Rural sl. Rare.

lambing-down shop: An outback public house. Rural sl. Obs.

lamplighter: A type of cicada.

lane: A stock route which has fences on each side.

lannet: A **kip** (q.v.) with a slot cut in it to hold a double-headed or double-tailed penny.

larrikin: A street tough or hoodlum; a boisterous youth. This term is being replaced by **bodgie.** Derivations include **larrikinism, larrikiness.**

Larry, happy as: Completely happy or contented.

lash at, have a: To make an attempt at some task or activity.

leanaway: A drunkard.

leatherneck: A station rouseabout (q.v.). Rural sl.

legpull: A deception or hoax.

lemony: Angry, irritable. Esp. **go lemony at.**

leprosy: Cabbage.

lerp: A chemical substance derived from **lerpamyllum** or **lerpamillum,** secreted by **lerp insects** or **lerps;** one of the few aboriginal words that have places in scientific terminology. In its orig. use, **lerp** meant sweet and was applied by aborigines to the scale-like sugary or waxy secretions of most species of insects of the family Psyllidae.

leslie: A lesbian.

letter stick: See **message stick.**

lezo: A lesbian. See **chromo.**

ling: A stench.

lizard: A musterer of sheep. Rural sl.

lob, v.: To arrive (at a place). Whence, **lob in,** call at a place. Also, **lob on to,** to discover, to obtain usually through a stroke of good fortune.

Lochinvar, the: An old-time term for catching lubras to work gold and, of course, to perform other services. Rural sl.

log: Any person regarded contemptuously for his lack of ability, brains and energy.

lolly: A sweet. 2. Anything extremely simple to do or understand. 3. A trickster's victim. Criminal sl. 4. One who is timid or half-hearted. Esp. "one who commits a crime in company yet does not want to be 'in it' so far as risks are concerned." Criminal sl.

long paddock, the: The open road. Rural sl.

long sleever: A large drink, esp. a large drink of beer.

long-stopper: A look-out man; see **cockatoo** and **nit-keeper.**

longtail: Treacle. Rural sl.

Loo, the: Woolloomooloo, Sydney.

loppy: A station **rouseabout** (q.v.). Rural sl.

lowheel: A prostitute. 2. A deadbeat.

lube: A drink, esp. a drink of beer.

lubra: A young woman. Borrowed from the aboriginal. 2. (In cards) a yarborough, i.e., a hand with no court cards.

lug someone's ear: To borrow money from someone. cf. **earlugger.**

lunatic soup: Cheap wine.

lurk: A dodge, scheme, racket. Whence, **lurk artist, lurkman(ship).**

lyre-bird, bit of a: A person who is prone to tell lies.

M

Ma State, the: New South Wales. Obs.

mad, get out your: To become incensed or angry.

mad as . . . : Many similes are used in Aust. to express ideas of silliness or stupidity, e.g., **mad as a beetle, mad as a cut snake, mad as a snake, mad as a Chinaman, mad as a dingbat, mad as a goanna, mad as a gumtree full of galahs** (cf. **galah**)**, silly as a curlew, silly as a two-bob watch, silly as a wet hen.**

mad dog: An unpaid score at a public house.

maggoty: Angry, peevish, irritable.

magpie: A South Australian.

mainlander: A person living on the Aust. continent, in contrast to one living in Tasmania, Papua or an offshore island.

make a box of: To confuse an issue, to cause a turmoil in some undertaking. See **box.**

make a sale: To vomit.

mallee root: A prostitute. A rhyme, influenced by the vulgar use of **root** (q.v.).

mana: Power, authority, prestige. (From the Maori.)

man with no hands, like a: Said of a mean or miserly person, esp. **throw money round like a man with no hands.**

Maoriland: New Zealand. Whence, **Maorilander,** a New Zealander.

marble, pass in one's: To die.

marjie: Marihuana.

mark, v.: To geld male lambs. The procedure on such occasions also usually involves the cutting of tails and marking of ears. Rural sl.

mark, get a (of a publican): To be fined for allowing betting or after-hours drinking.

Massey Harris: Cheese — "the greatest binder in the world."

mate, mateship: These words are Standard English in all the senses used in Aust., although they are probably used more often in Aust. than elsewhere. The main Aust. contribution has been in sentimentalising the terms.

matilda: A **bluey** or **swag** (q.v.). Whence, **carry matilda** and **waltz matilda,** to hump a bluey, to be a swagman.

mazuma: Money, esp. money that is used for betting.

meadow mayonnaise: Nonsense, "bullsh." See **bulldust, cowyard confetti,** etc.

merino, pure: Orig. a free settler in Aust. Later, members of the alleged "leading families." Later still, as an adj., first-class, superlative in quality.

message stick: A piece of wood bearing certain cuts or marks which serves as an aboriginal carrier's passport in hostile country. It is generally from 3 in. to 1 ft. long. The formalised symbols marked on it are believed to have some "meaning," but this point has not yet been clarified. Also, **letter stick.**

metho: Methylated spirits. Whence, **metho addict** or **metho artist,** one who drinks methylated spirits. 2. **Metho:** a Methodist.

mia-mia: A small, roughly built hut or shelter.

micky: A young, unbranded steer. Rural sl.

middy: A glass containing 10 oz. of beer. Mainly N.S.W. use.

migro: A migrant, esp. a migrant who arrived in this country after World War II.

milk bar: A shop or counter where milk drinks are sold. Whence, the economists' use of **milk bar economy** to denote "the tendency of non-essential consumer goods industries to expand beyond the capacity of basic industry to supply them with their raw material."

mimi art: A form of aboriginal cave painting, developed in Arnhem Land; according to the natives it was the work of **mimi**, a fairylike people with long, thin bodies who are capable of vanishing into the cracks of rocks. See **X-ray art.**

miner's right: A licence to dig for gold granted to a miner, orig. in the 1850s. See **joe!** etc.

mintie, without a: Penniless.

miserable as a bandicoot: Depressed in spirit. Also, **miserable as a shag on a rock.**

mix it: To fight (with someone).

mizzle, v.: To complain, grizzle.

mob: Any large number or quantity of persons, animals or things.

mock: A halfpenny.

mocker on, put the: To jinx, bring bad luck to. Also, **put the mock(s) on.**

moity (of wool): Carrying vegetable matter other than burr.

moleskin squatter: A working man who has come to own a small sheep-run. Rural sl. Obs. See **dungaree settler.**

money-spinner: A project that makes a lot of money; a racehorse that wins consistently.

monkey: A sheep. Whence, **monkey dodger,** a sheep-station hand; **monkey dodging,** sheep tending. Rural sl.

month of Sundays, as dull (slow) as a: Exceedingly dull or tiresome.

monty: A lie.

mopey as a wet hen: Depressed, low in spirits.

more hair on your chest! Good on you! A phrase of general encouragement and approval, mainly used by man to man.

morepork: A simpleton, a dull-witted person. Mainly rural sl.

Moreton Bay: Any court witness who lays an information, anyone who unwarrantably attends to or meddles in the affairs of others. Also, **Mor(e)ton Bay fig.** By rhyme on **gig** (q.v.). See also **fizgig.** Mainly criminal sl.

Moscow: A pawnshop. Whence, **to Moscow,** to pawn; **gone to Moscow,** pawned.

mossie, mozzie: A mosquito.

mote, v.: To hurry, travel rapidly.

motherer: A shepherd. Rural sl. Rare.

motser: A large sum of money. Sometimes **motza.**

mott, v.: To look at, stare at. cf. **gig.**

moz, v.: To interrupt, hinder. Whence, **to put the moz on someone,** to inconvenience a person. Also, **to mozzle.**

muck up, v.: To play the goat, to "play up." Whence, **mucker-up** and **mucking up.**

mud, up to: No good, worthless.

muffy: A frill-necked lizard.

mug cop: An opprobrious term for a policeman. Also, **mug copper** and **mug john.**

mug lair: See **lair.**

mulga: A rumour, a falsehood. Whence, **mulga wire,** a reputed source of rumour; **come over the mulga,** said of a rumour.

mulga madness: Queerness developed in lone bushmen or **hatters** (q.v.).

mullet: See **stunned mullet.**

mulligans: Cards.

mullock: Unwanted spoil or rock from a mine. 2. Any loose soil or rock from an excavation. 3. Something valueless.

mullock at, poke: To tease, jeer at, taunt. cf. **poke borak at.**

mullock over, v.: To work shoddily.

Murrumbidgee jam: Brown sugar moistened with cold tea and spread on **damper** (q.v.). Rural sl. Obs.

Murrumbidgee waler: A tramp who lived on the New South **WALES** side of the Murrumbidgee River at

a time when north of the river was known as
Sydneyside (q.v.) and the south as the **other side** or
Yarraside.

muscateer: An addict of muscat, esp. of the cheapest
kind.

my oath! A mild exclamation used esp. as a synonym for
Yes! or Of course!

my 'king oath! A vulgar variant of **my oath!**

myxo: The disease myxomatosis, used to kill rabbits in
large numbers.

N

nanny: A nannygai, a type of fish.

nark: Any unpleasantly disposed person. Also, **to nark,**
to foil, annoy; **narky,** irritable, ill-tempered.

nasty piece of work: An opprobrious phrase specifically
applied to an unpleasant person.

Naussie: A N(ew) Aussie; see **New Australian.**

neck, get under (someone's): To outwit or anticipate a
person.

neck, have a: To be impudent or cheeky; to be out-
rageous in a request.

Ned: Nickname inevitably given to any man named
Kelly.

Ned Kelly: See **Kelly, Ned.**

Ned Kelly, game as: See **game as Ned Kelly.**

nelly: Cheap wine.

never country, never land: See **never never.**

never never: Desert lands or remote areas in the far outback of Aust. Also, **never country** and **never land.**

New Australian: A recent migrant to Aust., esp. from
Britain or the European Continent. Sometimes
Naussie.

new chum: An immigrant. Whence, **newchumhood** and
newchumism. All obs. 2. A novice. As adj., inexpert.

new hand: As for **new chum,** 1. Obs.

New South: New South Wales.

nick, do a: To decamp, slip away unnoticed. Also, **nick
off.**

night fossick: To steal gold at night. Whence, **night-fossicking.** Rural sl. Obs. See **fossick.**

nit: A simpleton or fool; "half a nitwit."

nit, keep: To stand guard, keep watch, esp. while some illegal activity is afoot. See next:

nitkeep, v.: To stand guard. As n., one who stands guard.

nitkeeper: A person who keeps guard while illegal activity is afoot. cf. **cockatoo, 2.**

no good to gundy: No good at all. Sometimes, **no good to gundybluey** and **no good to gunty.**

no-hoper: A person without merit; a deadbeat; a person unworthy of confidence.

nobbler: A small drink of spirits. Whence, **nobblerise.** Obs.

no flies about (of a person): Wide awake, alert.

nong: A simpleton or fool. Also, **nong-nong.**

nose, on the: Unpleasant, objectionable. 2. Stinking. See **bugle, on the.**

not nominated: To have no chance of success.

not worth a cracker: Worthless.

not worth a cupful of cold water: Worthless. The word "cupful" is usually replaced by a vulgarism. Also, **not worth a pinch of ——.**

nowler: A sheep difficult to shear because of burr and dirt in the wool. Rural sl.

nuggety: Short, thickset, sturdy, stocky.

nulla nulla: An aboriginal club.

O

O.P., an: A borrowed cigarette, i.e., Other People's.

O.T.: The Overland Telegraph line running across central Aust. from Adelaide to Darwin, opened in 1872.

oddie: A halfpenny.

off one's bike, get: See **bike, get off one's.**

off the land, live: Used of a swagman's method of existence. Ironic, not only in contrast with authentic living "on the land," but in reference to what tramps extracted from homesteads. Obs.

off one's . . . : Used in many phrases to indicate stupidity or eccentricity, e.g., **off one's cadoova, off one's pannikin, off one's tile, off one's top, off one's saucer.** See **mad as . . .**

offsider: A friend, a follower, a partner, a hanger-on.

oil: Information, the true facts, an accurate tip. See **dinkum oil.**

oil up, v.: To advise, tip off.

old chum: An experienced bushman, miner, settler or worker in Aust., esp. one who has migrated from Britain. Obs. See **new chum.**

Old Country, the: Britain, esp. England. See **Home.**

Old Dart, the: Britain.

old identity: See **identity, old.**

old man, adj.: Mature, adult, extremely strong, as in **old man kangaroo, old man koala, old man possum;** also, **old man southerly,** a strong southerly wind. 2. As n., an elder of an aboriginal tribe.

old thing, the: A meal of **damper** (q.v.) and mutton. Rural sl.

on: Used for "at" or "in" when applied to a goldfield. A miner was always **on** Bendigo, **on** Ballarat, etc., never **at** those places. 2. (Of two people) in love. Also, **on with** (of one person in relation to another), in love with.

on at, to be: To scold, reprove, nag at.

oner: An amusing or eccentric person. Pronounced "wunner."

onkus: All wrong, incorrect; (of machinery) out of order. Sometimes, **honkus.**

onkey: Stinking. See **honk.**

only a rumour! Not half! Of course!

on one's pat: Alone. Truncated from the rhyming sl. **on one's pat malone.**

on the grouter: See **grouter.**

on the kelly: See **kelly,** 2.

on the outer: (To be) penniless, unwanted.

on the sheep's back: A phrase often applied to the Aust. economy.

on the tiger: (To be) engaged in a hard drinking bout.

on the wallaby (track): See **wallaby, on the.**

oodle: Money.

oozle, v.: To steal, to obtain by underhand means.

oscar: Money, ready cash.

our 'arbour: Port Jackson, N.S.W.

out, v.: To dismiss, reject, suspend. Esp. in past tense **outed.**

out of the wool: Said of sheep that have just been shorn. Rural sl.

out to it: Dead drunk; asleep.

outback: The back-country, the bush in general. Also, adj.

outrun: A sheep run at a considerable distance from the head station. Rural sl.

outside, the: Unsettled districts in the interior or bush. Whence, **outsider,** a person living in the **outback** (q.v.).

outstation: A sheep or cattle station remote from the head station. Rural sl.

over the board: (To be) in charge of a woolshed at shearing time. Rural sl.

overland, v.: To travel overland; to drive stock across country. Whence, **overlander,** a man who droves sheep, cattle or other stock long distances across country; **overlanding,** long-distance droving. Rural sl.

P

pack, go to the: To collapse (in a figurative sense); to lose one's morale; to go to pieces in the face of adversity. See **crack hardy.**

pack 'em: (To be) frightened, timid. Whence, **packing 'em.**

Paddo: The district of Paddington, Sydney. See **Darlo, Kenso.**

paddock: Any fenced area of grazing land, not as in Standard English, necessarily small. The use is often specified by such combinations as **cow paddock, home paddock, horse paddock,** etc. Whence, **to paddock,** to enclose grazing land with fences, to put stock in a paddock.

pakapoo ticket, marked like a: Confusedly or incomprehensibly marked.

pannikin boss: A minor overseer.

parcel: As for **swag** (q.v.).

parrot: As for **cocky, 2.**

part up, v.: To pay.

pastoralist: One who lives by keeping sheep or cattle; a **squatter** (q.v.); any landowner engaged in a primary industry involving the raising of stock.

pat, on one's: See **on one's pat.**

patch, on the: In trouble, "on the carpet."

pea: A racehorse that is being ridden to win, esp. where there is doubt about the genuineness of other runners.

peacock, v.: To select choice land in a district; **to pick the eyes out of** an area of farming land. Whence, **peacocking,** the practice. Obs. 2. To outwit or outsmart.

pea-dodger: A bowler hat.

peanutter: A person who grows peanuts.

peb: A larrikin (q.v.). See next:

pebble: A person (occasionally a horse) hard to control. Whence, **game as a pebble,** extremely courageous. 2. A **larrikin** (q.v.) or street hoodlum. Obs.

peg, n.: Something good, excellent, e.g., **it's a peg!** it's first-class!

peg, v.: To throw, as in **peg a gooly,** throw a stone.

peg, on the: In trouble, "on the carpet."

penner: A station hand who confines sheep in woolshed pens at shearing time. Also, **penner-up.** Rural sl.

perform: To swear luridly, to give way to temper. See **bung on an act.**

perish, do a: To suffer greatly from thirst, hunger or

destitution; esp. in the remote outback, to suffer thirst. Whence, **perishing track,** a route of outback travel where there is little or no water.

perk, v.: To vomit.

perve, v.: In Aust. sl. this word is almost exclusively applied to men. However, in spite of unfavourable connotations given to the term abroad, its use here often involves no more than watching a girl or woman in admiration. Whence, **to perve at** (a girl), to extract pleasure from looking at her, esp. if she is scantily dressed as on a beach.

peter: A cash register or till. Whence, **tickle the peter,** to rob a till. 2. A prison cell.

peter peter: A type of cicada.

phizgig: See **fizgig.**

piccaninny, adj.: Small. **Piccaninny daylight,** dawn. Also, n., an aboriginal baby or young child.

picked before he was ripe: Said of a person who is undersized or rawly innocent.

picker-up: A station hand who gathers shorn fleeces in a woolshed. Rural sl. 2. The man who picks up the coins in **two-up** (q.v.) and calls them when they have fallen.

pick the eyes out of: To select the best land in a grazing district. See **peacock.** Obs. 2. To select the best from any group of choices.

picnic: Any unpleasant experience; a disagreeable and complicated task. Esp. in negative form, **no picnic,** used to denote some unpleasant or disagreeable job.

pie: A combination of woolbuyers.

pie at: Expert at. Also, **pie on.**

pie eater: Contemptuous term for a person; someone of no importance.

piebald pony: A half-caste aboriginal child.

pierced dollar: As for **holey dollar** (q.v.).

pig islands: New Zealand. Whence, **pigislander,** a New Zealander.

pigs! A derisory or contemptuous exclamation. Often **pig's arse!**

piker: A wild bullock. Rural sl. 2. A trickster or confidence man.

Pilgrims: The first settlers in Canterbury, N.Z. N.Z. sl. Obs.

pin, v.: To have (someone) set, to have a grudge against.

pinch it off! Hurry up!

pink-eye: Ophthalmia suffered by stock in the outback, sometimes by humans. See **sandy blight.**

pipe: A scurrilous paper, a pasquinade lampooning high officials and well-known persons. Obs.

pirate: A man who picks up casual feminine company. Whence, **to pirate** and **on the pirate,** on the lookout for casual feminine company.

pissant around, v.: To waste time, dawdle, "mess about."

pit: A pocket.

placer: A sheep which attaches itself to a certain spot. Rural sl.

plant, v.: To hide stolen cattle or horses. Whence, **planter,** a cattle thief, **planting,** stock thieving. Rural sl. 2. (Of a horse) to remain perfectly still.

platypussery: A pen or specially prepared area in which platypuses are kept. Also, **platypussary.**

play the piano (of a shearer): To run one's fingers over the backs of sheep to find the easiest to shear. Rural sl.

plonk: Cheap wine; sometimes wine in general. See **bombo.**

plonkdot: A wine addict, esp. if female; a regular patron of a wine saloon.

plonk down, v.: To put down heavily. Also, **plonk (plank) one's frame down,** to sit down.

plonk out, v.: To pay, distribute money.

pluck, n.: A stone.

pluck a brand: To fake a new brand on stolen cattle or horses by pulling out the hairs around the existing brand. Rural sl.

plug hat: A bowler hat.

poached egg: A yellow-coloured "silent cop" placed at an intersection to guide traffic.

poddy, n.: A hand-fed calf, lamb or foal. Whence, **poddy-calf,** a hand-fed calf. Also, v., to rear a calf, lamb or foal by hand feeding.

poddy-dodger: A person who steals unbranded calves. Whence, **poddy-dodging,** the practice. Rural sl.

point, v.: To take an unfair advantage (of a person); to loaf, to impose on, to malinger. Whence, **pointer** and **pointing.**

poke, v.: To hit a person with the fist. Also, n., a blow with the fist. Often **take a poke at,** to strike someone.

poke borak at, poke mullock at: See **borak** and **mullock.**

poled: Stolen.

pole on: To impose on.

polers: Horses or bullocks harnessed alongside the pole of a waggon or dray. Rural sl.

poley: A de-horned or hornless cow, bull, bullock. Rural sl.

Polwarth: An Aust. breed of sheep first developed in the 1880s. The Polwarth is a **comeback** (q.v.).

pom: A Briton, esp. an English migrant to Aust.

pommy: A Briton, esp. an English migrant to Aust. Often abbreviated to **pom. Pommy bastard** is a frequent combination. cf. **jimmy.**

pong: A Chinese. 2. A stench.

ponk: A stench. Also, v., to smell offensively. cf. **honk** and **pong,** 2.

pony: A 5 oz. glass of beer. Also, **lady's waist.** N.S.W. sl.

pood: An effeminate male.

poofter: A male homosexual. Whence, **poofter rorter,** one who procures for a male homosexual.

poon: A lonely, somewhat crazy dweller in the outback. See **hatter.** 2. A simpleton or fool.

poon up, v.: To dress, esp. in ostentatious fashion. See **lair up.**

poor as a bandicoot: Extremely poor. See **bandicoot.**

poor man's diggings: Alluvial gold deposits, i.e., gold

which a poor man can work without capital. See
diggings. Rural sl.

pop: An attempt, a trial, e.g., **give him a pop.** Also, **have
a pop at,** to essay some undertaking.

poque: A purse, a pocket.

Port Phillip wool: High-quality wool produced in
Victoria.

possie: A place, position.

possum: A trickster's victim. Also, **poss** and **possodelux.**
Criminal sl.

possum guts: A coward, a weakling.

possum up a gumtree, like a: Completely happy.

post-and-rails tea: Strong billy tea. Rural sl.

pot on, put someone's: To betray a person, focus blame
on another. cf. **dob in.**

pozzie: As for **possie.**

prat one's frame in: To interfere, butt in.

Presbo: A Presbyterian.

Prince Alberts: Foot or toe rags as worn by impoverished
swagmen and other itinerants. Obs.

promote: To borrow or scrounge (something).

prop (of a horse): To come to a sudden halt, esp. when
travelling at a fast rate.

Prophets, the: Aust. settlers who went to Canterbury,
N.Z., in 1851. N.Z. sl. Obs. See **Pilgrims.**

prossie: A prostitute.

protected (of a person): Phenomenally lucky; one who is
tinny (q.v.).

proverbial, the: A bad mistake, esp. **come the proverbial,**
to meet one's Waterloo.

pull on: To undertake. As a male reference to a woman,
to marry. See **drag on.**

pull the weight: To meet a financial contingency.

pull your head in! Shut up! Mind your own business!
Also, **pull your skull in!**

punisher: A person who talks at excessive length. Also,
ear punisher. See **earbasher** and **wax borer.**

pure merino: See **merino, pure.**

push: A gang, clique, social group.

push the knot: To carry a swag; to travel as a swagman.

put the cleaners through: To borrow from (a person); to "take down" (a person).

put the nips in: To ask (someone) for a loan; to "bite" a person. Also, **put the fangs in** and **put the bee on.** cf. **stick it into.**

putty, up to: Worthless, of no importance. Equivalents are **up to mud** and **up to tripe.**

Pyrmont Yank: As for **Woolloomooloo Yank** (q.v.).

Q

Q fever: A type of fever, in which delirium is common, first described by E. H. Derrick in Queensland in 1937.

quailer: A stone.

quaky isles, the: New Zealand.

quart pot: A large tin pot or billy (q.v.) used for boiling water or cooking in the bush. Rural sl.

queen up (of a male): To get dressed, esp. for a festive occasion, although not necessarily in an effeminate fashion as the word **queen** (or **quean**) suggests. See **lair up, poon up.**

quince: An effeminate male; a stupid person.

quince, to get on one's: To annoy or anger. cf. **get on one's tit, get on one's works.**

quoits, go for one's: To hurry, travel rapidly.

R

rabbit: A bottle of beer. cf. **run the rabbit.**

rafferty rules: No rules at all. Applied to any system, organisation or contest run in slipshod fashion. Sometimes **rafferty's rules.**

rager: A wild, unruly bullock that causes disturbance in a stockyard. Rural sl.

raker, go a: To fall heavily, come a "cropper."

ram: A trickster's confederate. cf. **amsterdam, bumper-up.** Criminal sl.

ram-struck mutton: Tough meat from old ewes past breeding. Rural sl.

raspberrylander: A Tasmanian. Obs. See **Apple Island(er).**

ratbag: An eccentric person. Whence, **ratbaggery,** eccentricity.

raw prawn, come the: To attempt to deceive or hoodwink (someone).

razoo: A non-existent coin, sometimes **brass razoo.** Esp. used negatively as in "I haven't a **razoo,**" I haven't any money. See **skerrick.**

razorbacks: Cattle that are lean and scraggy. Rural sl.

ready, n.: A swindle, a conspiracy. Esp. **a ready-up.** Also, **work a ready,** to cheat. 2. **The ready,** money, ready cash.

ready up, v.: To tip off; to put someone wise.

red 'arry: A £10 note. Also **brick.**

red centre, the: The central area of Aust.

redeye: A type of cicada.

red ned: Cheap red wine.

reds: Fleas.

red steer, the: A bushfire.

reef off: To take (esp. to take money) from a person, e.g., **reef it off in lumps,** to extract large sums of money from someone.

reffo: A refugee from Europe who—just before or just after World War II — settled in Aust. cf. **New Australian.**

removalist: A person or firm engaging in the shifting of household or business effects.

remittance man: A Briton living in Aust. on money sent to him more or less regularly from his country.

ribuck: Correct, genuine. Obs.

ridge: Satisfactory, genuine, approved. Also, **ridgey-didge, ridgey-dig.**

right oil: Correct information, the true facts. cf. **dinkum oil.**

righto! Yes! Okay! 2. That's enough! Break it down!

ring: The scene of operations of a two-up school or the school itself.

ring a shed: To shear the largest number of sheep in a shearing shed; to be the best shearer in the shed. See **ringer,** 1. Rural sl.

ring dollar: As for **holey dollar** (q.v.).

ringneck: A jackeroo (q.v.). Rural sl.

ring of: Remarkably alike (a person). Whence, **dead ring of.**

ring one's tail: To submit, give in, reveal timidity.

ringer: The fastest shearer in a shearing shed. Rural sl. 2. A person of outstanding competence in a job. 3. A stockman. Rural sl.

ringie: The keeper of a two-up school.

ringtail: A coward. cf. **ring one's tail.**

riverina: A shilling; by rhyme on **deaner.** Rare.

roar (of cattle): To low continuously as when restless. Whence, **roaring,** the noise so made. A horse which makes a loud sound when breathing is said to **roar.** Rural sl.

roaring horsetails: The Aurora Australis. Rare.

rock-hopper: A person who fishes from rocks on a sea coast.

rocky: A rock wallaby. 2. A rockmelon.

rod in pickle: Said of a good racehorse that is being held for a certain win.

roll! go and have a: Go to the devil! Go away!

roll-up, n.: An assembly or gathering; the number of people attending a meeting.

roo: A kangaroo.

root, v.: To outwit, baffle, exhaust, utterly confound (someone). Whence, **to be rooted,** to be exhausted or confounded; **get rooted!** Go to blazes!

ropeable: Violently angry; savagely ill-tempered.

rort: A dodge, scheme or racket. 2. A lively, esp. a drunken, party; an orgy.

rosella: A sheep that has lost part of its wool. Rural sl.

rotten: Drunk.

rotten form! how's your: How lucky you are!

rough, a bit: Unreasonable, unfair.

rough as bags: Unpolished, crude, coarse. Also, **rough as a bag, rough as a pig's breakfast, rough as guts, rough as goat's knees.**

rough off (a horse): To break in crudely, esp. for station work. Rural sl.

rough on: Hard on, severe towards (a person).

rough-up, n.: A fight, a street brawl.

roughy: An example of sharp dealing or victimisation.

rouse on: To upbraid (a person), reprove, "tell off." Also, **get roused on.**

rouseabout: A handyman on a station. Whence, a handyman in any job. **Blackfellow's rouseabout,** a nobody.

roust on: As for **rouse on.**

roziner: A strong alcoholic drink. Also spelt **rozner.**

rubberdy: A hotel. Also, **rubbity** and **rubby.** Mutilated rhyme **rub-a-dub-dub** on "pub."

rug: A £1 note.

rumour: See **only a rumour!**

run: A station; a large area of grazing land. Often in the combinations **cattle run** and **sheep run.**

run a sheep: To shear a sheep's fleece near the top, leaving the thick base wool intact. Rural sl.

run, get the: To be dismissed from employment. Also, **give the run to** (someone).

run the rabbit: To secure liquor, often illegally, e.g., after hours. See **rabbit.**

run rings around: To defeat (someone) soundly in any contest of skill or intelligence. See **ringer.**

runabouts: Cattle allowed to graze freely. Rural sl.

Russians: Wild horses or wild cattle. Rural sl. Rare.

rybuck: As for **ribuck.**

S

S.P.: Starting Price (off course) betting. Whence, **S.P. book, S.P. bookmaker, S.P. shop, S.P. joint.**

sand blight: See **sandy blight.**

sandgroper: A Western Australian. Whence, **sand-groping,** living in W.A. See **groper, groperland.**

sandscratch, v.: To search for surface gold. Rural sl. 2. To be on the lookout for a feminine companion.

sandy blight: A form of ophthalmia in which the eyes feel as though there is sand in them. Also, **sand blight.**

sane: Ten, i.e., 10 months' jail, 10 oz. tobacco. Esp. criminal sl. but note that 10 years' jail or £10 is most commonly a **brick.** 2. A 10s. note.

sanno: A sanitary inspector. cf. **garbo.**

say-so, n.: A leader, boss.

scale, v.: To ride on a public conveyance without paying a fare. Whence, **scaling,** the practice. 2. To steal; to rob (a person).

scaler: One who rides on a public conveyance without paying a fare. 2. A thief, a swindler. cf. **scale, v.** 2.

school of arts: Usually no more than a combination of meeting hall and rough library found in many rural townships. The first School of Arts was opened in Sydney in 1833.

schooner: A 15 oz. glass of beer. N.S.W. 2. A smaller glass of beer in South Aust.

scrub, n.: Bush, any bush-covered area of land.

scrub, v.: To reject, dismiss.

scrub cattle: Cattle that have run wild in scrub or bush. Rural sl.

scrub cocky: A small farmer working rough land or an area largely covered with bush. Rural sl. See **cocky.**

scrub dangler: A wild bullock. Rural sl.

scrub-dashing: Riding through bush or scrub, esp. after strayed cattle or horses. Rural sl.

scrubbers: Cattle or horses that have run wild in the scrub and have deteriorated in condition. Rural sl.

scrum: A 3d. coin.

secko: A person suffering a sexual aberration.

second cuts: See **fribby.**

seed tick: The larval stage of the cattle tick. Rural sl.

selector: A farmer who took Crown Land and acquired the freehold by annual payments. Whence, **to select land** and **selection.**

send her down Hughie! An exclamation of approval when rain falls. **Hughie** here stands for the deity.

settler's matches: Long, pendulous strips of bark hanging from eucalypts which are readily ignited and used as kindling. Rural sl.

Shagroons: Aust. squatters who invaded Canterbury, N.Z., in 1851-2. Obs. See **Pilgrims** and **Prophets.**

shakey isles, the: New Zealand. Also, **quaky isles.**

shanghai, n.: A child's catapult. Also, v., to shoot with a shanghai. See **ging, gogeye, shot-ging, shong.**

sharp shooter: A person who mingles with a racecourse crowd round a bookmaker's stand, holds out his hand and demands a ticket for a non-existent bet. Also, **sharp shooting,** the practice.

shears, off the (of sheep): Animals that have just been shorn. Rural sl. See **in the wool.**

shed: As for **woolshed.**

sheep-sick, adj.: Used to describe pasture which is (temporarily, at least) unsuitable for carrying sheep; land upon which sheep have been grazed too long. Rural sl.

sheep station: A large pastoral property where sheep are grown for wool or meat. Use of the term is often confined to the homestead area; hence **out sheep station. Station** and **run** are interchangeable.

sheila: A girl or young woman.

shelf: A police informer. Also, **shelfer.** cf. **fizgig, topoff.**

shepherd: A miner who holds a gold claim, but does not work it. Rural sl.

shicer: An unproductive gold mine. Obs. See **shyster.** 2. A swindler or crook. 3. A racecourse welsher.

shick: Drunk. Also, **shicked.**

shicker, v.: To drink. Whence, **get shickered,** to get drunk. As n., a drunkard. Also, **on the shicker,** said of a person who is drinking heavily.

shift, v.: To travel at great speed. Also, n., **do a shift,** to move, decamp.

shin off, v.: To leave hurriedly. Also, **do a shin.**

shingle short, have a: To be stupid or crazy. Rare.

shiralee: A swag or bluey (q.v.).

shivoo: A party, a spree. Also, **shivaroo.**

shivy (of wool): Carrying small, fine particles of vegetable matter.

shong: A child's catapult.

shook on: (To be) keen on, interested in, infatuated with.

shoot through: To decamp; to leave unexpectedly; (of a Serviceman) to go A.W.L. Whence, **shoot through like a Bondi tram.** Also, **go through.**

short: Silly, stupid; esp. **a bit short.** cf. **shingle short.** Also, **short of a sheet (of bark).**

shot-ging: A child's catapult.

shouse: A privy.

shout, n.: A free drink or a free round of drinks. Whence, one's turn to buy drinks for another. Also, one's turn to pay for anything, e.g., tickets for a cinema.

shout, v.: To buy drinks for another or for others. Whence, **shouting,** the practice. Also, to pay for entertainment for another.

shove it! A contemptuous ejaculation of dismissal. See **stick it!**

shove off: To depart.

shower: A dust storm—as in **Cobar shower, Bedourie shower, Darling shower, Wilcannia shower,** etc. Rural sl.

shyster: A crook, a humbug.

sick as a blackfellow's dog: Extremely ill.

sidekick: A friend, companion, helper. cf. **offsider.**

silvertail: A member of the upper crust; a social climber.

sing a bone: As for **bone,** v.

sit down: To camp or settle (at a place); to **squat.**

sit up like Jacky: See **Jacky.**

sixty-miler: A collier which transports coal from Newcastle to Sydney.

skerrick: A small amount or small quantity of anything;

a small sum of money. Esp. used negatively, e.g., he hasn't a skerrick, he's penniless; **he hasn't a skerrick of** (some specified item), he hasn't any; **not a skerrick left,** nothing remains.

skite, n.: A braggart, a boaster. Also, **skiter.**

skite, v.: To brag, boast, show off. Whence, **skiting.**

sleever: A drink, esp. a large drink. See **long sleever.**

sling: A tip (money). Also, **to sling,** to tip.

sling off: To depart. cf. **shove off.**

sling off at: To deride, jeer at (a person).

slip-up: A deliberately missed appointment.

sly-grog: A place where sly-grog is sold. Also, **sly-groggery.**

smoke-oh: A spell from work, a short period of rest. Also, **smoke-o.**

smoodge, v.: To make love to; to kiss; to flatter. Also, **smoodge up to** (someone).

smoodger: A sycophant, a flatterer.

snack: A certainty. 2. A prospective victim for a swindle or robbery. Criminal sl.

snags: Sausages.

snailey: A bullock with a slightly twisted horn. Rural sl.

snatch it: To leave a job; to abandon a task. Also, **snatch one's time.**

snob: The last sheep shorn in a day's work in a woolshed. Also called a **cobbler.** Rural sl.

snoot, n.: A disagreeable person.

snoozer: A young child.

snork: A baby. 2. A sausage.

snorkers: Sausages. See **snags.**

snorter: A particularly hot day.

snout on, have a: To bear a grudge against (a person); to have "a set against" (someone). Whence, **sore as a snouted sheila,** as angry as a girl who has been exposed to some indignity.

soak: "A depression holding water after rain." 2. A waterhole. Both rural.

soakage: As for **soak.**

sod: A **damper** (q.v.), esp. a badly cooked damper. Rural sl.

soda: A certainty; an easily accomplished task.

solid: Unfair, unreasonable. Esp. **a bit solid.**

sonky: Stupid, silly.

sool, v.: To travel fast. 2. As for **sool on.**

sool on: To incite to attack, used esp. of a dog.

sort: A girl or young woman. See **good sort.** 2. By implication, a youth, as in "all the girls and their **sorts** are going to the pictures."

sort someone out: To reprove a person, put him in his place, fight him.

south, v.: To put (an object) in one's pocket. Also, **to dip south,** to search in one's pocket for money.

southerly buster: A wild wind or gale from the south. The form **southerly burster** is obs. 2. A mixed alcoholic drink.

souvenir, v.: To steal, purloin.

spare boy: Treacle or golden syrup. Rural sl.

spear, get the: To be dismissed from a job. Also, **give the spear,** to dismiss an employee.

speck, the: Tasmania. Also, **the fly speck.** Both rare.

speed the wombats! An exclamation. See **stone the crows!**

Speewaa: A legendary station of doughty deeds (the orig. Speewaa was near Swan Hill on the Murray River); a place of "great men and tall tales." Whence, **on the Speewaa.**

spell-oh: A period of rest. See **smoke-oh.**

spiel, n.: Set advice. 2. A wordy explanation.

spiel, v.: To talk plausibly or glibly, esp. with some underhand motive in view.

spieler: A swindler, welsher, card-sharp.

spin: £5. Also, **spinnaker.**

spine-basher: A loafer. Whence, **spine-bashing.**

spinner: The man who tosses the coins in two-up. Whence, the phrase, **come in spinner,** which is said when all bets have been set and the toss is required. 2. £50.

spit a bone at: See **bone, to** and **sing a bone.**

spit in the bag and stand up (of a penniless bookmaker): To seek bets from racecourse punters without the means to pay those bets if they are successful.

split: A safety match.

spot, n.: £10.

spot, v.: To choose the best land in a district, esp. at the expense of others. Rural sl. Obs. See **peacock.**

spridgy: A sparrow. Also, **sproggy** and **spudgy.**

sprook, spruik, v.: To harangue (said esp. of a sideshow-man), to appeal with glib tongue to prospective customers or victims.

sprooker, spruiker: A speaker; a voluble sideshowman.

square dinkum: True, vouched for, honest. cf. **fair dinkum.**

square off, v.: To apologise, explain, set matters right in a misunderstanding. Whence, **square-off,** n., an apology, excuse.

squat: To take up land as a **squatter** (q.v.). Obs. Also, **squattage,** a squatter's land; **squattocracy** and **squatterdom,** squatters collectively; **squatting,** pertaining to the activities of a squatter.

squatter: A large land-holder in the outback; the owner of a major **run** or **station** (q.v.).

squeaker: A type of cicada.

squib, n.: A cowardly person. Sometimes used negatively as in **his mother never raised a squib,** he is brave, willing to tackle any opponent or obstacle.

squib, v.: To funk, evade an issue, be afraid of some opponent or obstacle. Also, **squib on,** to betray (a person), to evade an issue.

squiz, v.: To look at, inspect. As n., an inspection.

stack on an act: As for **bung on an act.** See **bung, 2.**

stag: An imperfectly castrated ram. Whence, **staggy,** adj. 2. A half-grown bull. Both rural sl.

staggering bob: A calf. See **bobby calf.** Rural sl.

standing ground: The bottom of a goldmine shaft which needs no timbering. Rural sl. Obs.

standover (man): A criminal who exacts toll from other lawbreakers or innocents. Also, **standover merchant.**

standover, work the: To act as a **standover man.**

start, n.: A job.

station: While this term for a squatter's property is not orig. Aust., it is used far more often here than overseas. The following derivatives are Aust.: **back station, head station, home station, out station, outside station, station hand, station keeper,** etc.

steam: Cheap wine, esp. fortified wine.

steamer: A dish of stewed kangaroo flavoured with pork. Rural sl.

sterks, give one the: To infuriate, annoy, depress.

sterling: An English-born resident in Aust. Obs. See **currency.**

stew: A boxing contest, race or athletic event, the result of which has been pre-arranged.

stick, n.: An inquisitive person, truncated from **sticky-beak.** 2. A two-up **kip.** (q.v.).

stick it! A contemptuous ejaculation of dismissal. cf. **shove it!**

stick it into: To ask (someone) for a loan. cf. **put the nips in.**

stick-up, n.: A delay, a hold-up, a quandary. See next:

stick up, v.: Orig. to hold up and rob a person on the road or in the bush. Obs. 2. To delay, to stop.

sticky: Curious, inquisitive. cf. **stick, 1.** (As applied to weather) humid, muggy.

stiff, n.: A summons.

stiff, adj.: Short of, lacking in, e.g., **to be stiff for a few bob.** 2. Broke, penniless, as in **stiff as a crutch.** 3. Unlucky.

stiffen the lizards! stiffen the snakes! Exclamations equivalent to **stone the crows!** (q.v.).

stiffened, get: To be swindled, taken down. cf. **stiff, adj.**

sting, n.: Dope given to a racehorse, esp. in the form of a hypodermic injection. Whence, **give a sting to** (a horse), to dope it.

stinko: Drunk.

stitched: Beaten, outwitted.

stock: Farm animals in general, but esp. cattle. Whence, **stock route, stockman, stockyard, stock and station agent,** etc.

stone, adj.: An intensive, as in **stone moral,** a certainty, **stone motherless (broke),** penniless.

stone the crows! An exclamation mainly indicating exasperation or surprise. cf. **starve the bardies! stiffen the lizards!** etc.

stop laughing! This typical example of Aust. meiosis means: Stop complaining (or grousing)!

stop one: To take a drink of alcoholic liquor.

stoush, n.: A fight, a brawl, a thrashing, violence. Whence, **put in the stoush,** to fight vigorously, and **stoush-up,** a fight, a brawl. Also, v., to defeat in a fight, esp. **to stoush someone.**

straight oil: Correct information, the facts. cf. **dinkum oil.** Also, **straight wire.**

strap up: To obtain goods—esp. drinks in a hotel—on credit.

strength of, the: The real facts (about something). See next:

strong of, the: The real facts (about something); a full assessment of (a person).

strongarm, v.: To act as a protector, specifically for a prostitute. To act in a bullying fashion. Esp. **strong-arm tactics.**

stump-jumper: An Aust. farming implement known as a **stump-jump plough.** Whence, **stump-jumping,** work with such a plough. Rural sl.

stunned mullet, like a: Stupid, silly.

sudden: Speedy, drastic, brutal towards, as in **sudden death on.**

suint: Dried sweat of a sheep in its wool. Rural.

Sunday dog: A lazy dog of little use to a shepherd or cattle man. Rural sl.

sundowner: A rural tramp or **swagman** (q.v.) of indolent type who usually dodged working for his food by arriving at a station at sundown. Rare.

sunshine track, on the: (To be) on the tramp in the outback. Obs.

surfacing: Searching for gold on the surface of the ground. Rare.

surfing: Swimming in the sea. **Surf** derivatives are largely Aust. in origin and/or use, e.g., **surf patrol, surf boat, surf board, surf ski, surf club, surf reel, surf line, surf life saving, surfman, surf rider.**

susso: The dole; Government sustenance for the unemployed. Whence, **on the susso,** in receipt of the dole.

swag: A rolled blanket, within which are wrapped personal effects, carried by a rural tramp or swagman. Whence, **hump one's swag** and **to swag it.**

swaggie: A swagman.

swagman: A rural tramp who carries a **swag** or **bluey** (q.v.).

swamp, v.: To spend money, mainly on drink. Whence, **swamp down,** to swallow or gulp down (a drink). 2. See next:

swamper: An itinerant in the outback or bush who walked to his destination without his **swag** (q.v.), which he entrusted to a teamster to bring on his waggon. Obs. Also, **to swamp** and **to swamp it.**

sweat on: To wait, usually to wait anxiously (for something to happen).

sweat points: See **fribby.** Also, **sweat locks,** wool from the belly of a sheep, often matted with dirt and sweat. Rural sl.

sweeper: A train which stops at all stations on its route.

sweet, adj.: Ready, prepared, satisfied. Esp. **she's sweet,** everything is all right. (The "she" has no feminine connotation whatever either in this phrase or comparable expressions, such as, **she's apples, she's jake, she's ridge.**)

swing the gate: To be the fastest shearer in a woolshed, or merely to be a fast shearer. Rural sl.

swy: The game of two-up. Sometimes **swy-up.** 2. A florin, i.e., two shillings.

Sydney blanket: As for **Wagga blanket** (q.v.).

Sydney ducks: Australians who went to California in the 1849 gold rush. Obs.

Sydney harbour: A barber.

Sydney or the bush: The choice of a final alternative.

Sydneyside: Orig. that part of N.S.W. north of the Murray River. Obs. 2. The area in and around Sydney.

Sydneysider: Orig. a resident of the northern, Sydney side of the Murray, in contrast to the southerner or **Yarrasider.** Obs. 2. An inhabitant of Sydney.

Sydney View: A postage stamp issued in N.S.W. in 1850, the central feature of which is a copy of the reverse side of the first Great Seal of N.S.W., showing three convicts being freed from their chains. Also **View.**

T

take, n.: A swindler, one who defrauds or cheats.

take a piece out of: To reprove (someone) sharply.

take a screw at: To look at, examine.

take-down: A deception or fraud.

take-on, n.: A fight. Also, **to take (someone) on,** to engage a person in combat or in any contest of skill or endurance.

talent, the: Larrikins, bodgies, crooks, the underworld in general. 2. Females attending a party or gathering.

Tambaroora muster: A collection of money to buy drinks. Obs.

tank: An excavation (generally square) on a station in which water is held for stock. Whence, **tank-sinker,** a man who excavates a tank, and **tank-sinking.**

tarboy: A woolshed hand whose job at shearing time is to administer tar to cut sheep. Rural sl.

Tatts: Tattersall's lottery, Tasmania. Whence, **a ticket in Tatts.**

Tazzie: Tasmania; a Tasmanian. Sometimes spelt **Tassie.**

teaser: A castrated or partly castrated ram, which is placed in a ewe flock to identify ewes on heat. Rural sl.

teddy bear: A flashily dressed and exhibitionistic person. By rhyme on **lair** (q.v.).

ten, twelve, two and a quarter: "An old formula for a man's rations on farms and stations — 10 lb. flour, 12 lb. meat, 2 lb. sugar, ¼ lb. tea." Obs.

territorian: A resident in the Northern Territory. Also, but less often, a resident of other Government territories.

there's no doubt about you! A rather nonsensical phrase of admiration or goodwill.

three-cornered horse: A scraggy, weedy, outlaw horse. Rural sl.

three pen'orth of God help us: A contemptuous phrase applied to a weakling or an insignificant person.

threshing machine, fight like a: To fight vigorously.

throw-in: As for **chuck-in** (q.v.).

tickle the peter: To rob a cash register or till.

tick-stain: Discolouration of wool caused by excreta of the sheep "tick" or ked. Rural sl.

tie up a dog: To obtain credit for drinks at a hotel. Also, **chain up a pup.** An account which the debtor fails to pay is called a **mad dog.**

tiers: Mountains. Whence, **tiersman,** a person living in the mountains. Tasmanian sl.

tilda: As for **Matilda** (q.v.). Obs.

tinarse: An unusually lucky person. Whence, **tinarsed.** cf. **tinny** and **arsey.**

tin ear: An eavesdropper.

tin-kettling: A form of noise-making to celebrate some special occasion, which consists of banging tins, metal trays and other objects capable of producing a racket.

tinny: Unusually or fantastically lucky. See **tinarse.**

tipslinger: A racehorse or greyhound tipster.

tit, get on one's (of a situation or person): To annoy one greatly, to infuriate. cf. **get on one's works.**

ti-tree: Incorrect for **tea-tree.**

tiz up: As for **flossy up** (q.v.).

T.M., a: A ready made or Tailor Made cigarette.

toe rag: Orig. rags which an outback itinerant wound about his toes or feet. See **Prince Alberts, 2.** A person of small account; a **no-hoper** (q.v.). 3. A £1 banknote.

toe-ragger: A short-sentence prisoner in a jail. Criminal sl.

togs: A swimming costume. Often **swimming togs.** See **bathers.**

Tom Collins: The supposed source of rumour in the Riverina area. Obs. Name taken by author Joseph Furphy. See **furphy.**

tomahawk, v.: To cut a sheep during shearing. Rural sl.

tommy, n.: Bread baked with currants and sugar. Rural sl.

tommy, v.: To leave, decamp.

Tommy Cornstalk: An Aust. soldier in the Boer War. Obs. cf. **cornstalk** and **digger.**

tom thumb: A type of cicada.

tongs: Hand shears (for shearing sheep). Rural sl.

tonk: A simpleton or fool; an effeminate male.

tonked, get: To be knocked out, beaten in a fight; to be punished.

too right! Yes! Certainly!

topoff: A police informer. cf. **fizgig** and **shelf.**

Top End, the: Far northern Aust., esp. the Northern Territory. Whence, **Topender,** an inhabitant of the Far North.

tote: A racecourse totalisator.

tough as fencing wire: Extremely durable. Similarly, **tough as seasoned mulga, tough as ironbark.**

track: A warder who will carry contraband messages or goods out of or into jail for a prisoner. Criminal sl.

triantelope: Popular name for the large huntsman spider, Delèna cancerides. Also (but erroneously) called **tarantula.**

trot: A sequence. Esp. **bad trot,** a sequence of failures; **good trot,** a sequence of successes.

tucker: Food in general. Whence, **tuckerbag, tuckerbox, tuckertime.** See **dog, 1.**

turf out: To throw away, reject.

turps: Any alcoholic drink. Whence, **be on the turps** and **get on the turps.**

twicer: A double-crosser.

two-up: A gambling game in which two (occasionally three) pennies are tossed. Also called **swy, swy-up** and **heading 'em.**

U

undress a sheep: To shear a sheep. Rural sl.

uni: A university.

union jack: A type of cicada.

up: Up to specifications or up to standard. Used esp. in the negative, **not up,** no good, not up to expectations.

up a gumtree: In a quandary.

up country: The inland; the outback.

up King Street: Bankrupt, in financial difficulties. Sydney sl.

up there, Cazaly! A cry of encouragement. Cazaly was a noted South Melbourne footballer, whose specialty was high marking.

up to putty: No good, worthless. Also, **up to mud** and **up to tripe.**

upter: No good, worthless.

upya! A contemptuous ejaculation of rejection or indifference.

up you for the rent! As for **upya!**

urger: A racecourse tipster. 2. A trickster's confederate. Criminal sl.

V

Van Diemenese, Vandemonian: An inhabitant of Van Diemen's Land, the old name for Tasmania. Obs.

Vic.: Victoria.

View: See **Sydney View.**

V.J.: A 11½ ft. closed-deck sailboat, known as **Vaucluse Junior.**

V.S.: A 15½ ft. sailboat, known as **Vaucluse Senior.**

W

W.A.: Western Australia.

waddy: A wooden club, a stick.

Wagga blanket: A covering used by tramps, made by cutting open a chaff bag or flour sack and hemming it roughly. Also called **Sydney blanket.**

Wagga grip: A leather strap or binding through the pommel D's of a saddle. Also called **jug handle** and **monkey.**

wake-up, a: An alert person. Esp. used in "I'm a wake-up to you," I know what you're up to, you can't fool me.

waler: See **Murrumbidgee waler.** 2. A light type of horse used for Army purposes or any horse exported from **N.S. Wales.**

walkabout, go: To wander, to travel apparently aimlessly over long distances.

wallaby: An outback track. Esp. **on the wallaby,** tramping in the outback. Rural sl.

waltz Matilda: To carry a **swag** or **bluey** (q.v.). Whence, **waltzing Matilda,** tramping in the outback. The orig. form was **walking Matilda.**

warb: A low-paid manual worker. 2. A dirty or untidy person. 3. A simpleton or fool.

warby: Insecure, unwell. Esp. **to feel warby.**

warrigal: Anything wild or untameable. Also, adj., wild. See **yarraman.**

washerwoman: A type of cicada.

waterbag: A portable canvas container for water. 2. A teetotaller or temperance fanatic.

Watsons, bet like the: To bet large sums of money on a horse race.

wattle: A dirty or untidy person. Truncated from **wattle and daub,** rhyming sl. based on **warb** (q.v.).

wax borer: A person who talks drearily and at length. cf. **earbasher** and **punisher.**

weekender: A cottage or shack at some beach or bush resort where week-ends and holidays are spent.

Westralia: Western Australia. Whence, **Westralian,** n., an inhabitant of Western Aust.; adj., pertaining to Western Aust.

wet, n.: A simpleton or fool. Whence, **all wet,** stupid, wrong.

wet, get: To become angry.

wet, the: The rainy season in Australia's north from December to March. cf. **dry, the.**

whacko! Good! Hurrah! An ejaculation of pleasure or approval.

what do you know? A loose greeting which has little direct sense of enquiry about it. Also, **what do you know!** An exclamatory phrase of approval, mainly used ironically.

what it takes: Money, courage, stamina, ability.

what's this, bush week? A derisory phrase, usually indicating that the speaker is not deceived by another. Also, **what do you think this is—bush week?**

whinge, v.: To complain at length, to grouse, to whine. Sometimes used as n., as in **have a whinge.** Whence, **whinger,** a person who complains; **whingeing,** a complaint, the action of complaining.

whip the cat: To cry over spilt milk; to complain about misfortune, esp. when that misfortune is a product of one's own carelessness.

whisky drinker: A type of cicada.

white ant, v.: To undermine or sabotage, esp. in an industrial or political sense. Whence, **white-anter,** a saboteur; **white-anting,** sabotage.

who's robbing this coach! Mind your own business! Also, **who's milking this cat!**

widgie: The female companion of the **bodgie** (q.v.).

willy: A supply of betting money.

willy, throw a: To have a fit. Also, **chuck a willy.**

willy willy: A brief but wild dust storm of cyclonic type. Mainly experienced in the outback.

winge: See **whinge.**

wipe: To dispense with. **To wipe a person,** to refuse to have anything to do with that person.

witchetty: Edible (to aborigines) grublike larva of any of several species of longicorn beetle. Also, **witchetty grub.** There is doubt whether the word is aboriginal.

wog: A germ or parasite. Whence, **to have the wog,** to have influenza or some unexplained minor disease. 2. Anything small, a small piece of extraneous matter.

wommera: An aboriginal spear-throwing instrument.

wonk: A white man or white woman. Aborigines (esp. half-castes) use this pejorative much as whites use the word **boong** to denote an aboriginal.

wood on, have the: To have an advantage over (an opponent).

woolblind: Used to describe a sheep the eyes of which have become covered with long wool (merinos are common sufferers). Rural sl.

woolclasser: A dog which bites sheep. Rural sl.

woolscour: A shed where wool is washed.

woolshed: A large building on a sheep station where sheep are shorn. Also, **shed.**

Woolloomooloo Yank: A Sydney youth who imitates U.S. speech and habits in an effort to colour his personality. cf. **Pyrmont Yank.**

Woop Woop: The hypothetically most rustic of all rustic townships in Aust.

word, v.: "To accost with fair speech."

word up, v.: To advise, "tip off" a person.

works, get on someone's: To annoy, anger, infuriate a person.

wouldn't it! Exclamation of disgust or disapproval.

wowser: A killjoy, a blue-stocking, a puritan.

wurley: A rough hut.

X

X-ray art: A form of aboriginal bark and cave painting which shows internal parts of human and animal anatomy. See **mimi art.**

Y

yabber: To talk, chatter, gabble. Also, **have a yabber** (about something) **with** (someone).

yabbie: A small freshwater crayfish. Also, **yabby.** Whence, **to yabbie** and **to go yabbying.**

yacker: Hard work. Also, **yakker.**

yank, n.: As for next:

yankee shout: Fraternal drinking in which every man pays for himself. See **shout.**

yarra: Mad. Whence, **stone yarra,** completely mad.

Yarra bankers: Loafers and down-and-outs who dawdled away their days on the banks of the River Yarra, Melbourne. Obs. See **Domain dosser, Domain squatter.**

yarraman: An outlaw horse or wildly behaved station hack. Also called a **warrigal.** Rural sl.

Yarrasider: See **Sydneysider.**

yeller feller: An aboriginal half-caste.

yellow monday: A type of cicada. Orig. from an aboriginal name approximately rendered as **yellow-mundee.**

yellow tuesday: A type of cicada. See above.

yike: A row or argument, a fight.

yonnie: A small stone, a pebble.

you beaut! A phrase mainly used to denote approval, but often ironical. Also, **you little beauty!**

yow, to keep: To stand guard. As for **keep nit** (q.v.).

Z

zack: Sixpence.

ziff: A beard.